THE DESKTOP DIGEST

— of —

DESPOTS & DICTATORS

THE
DESKTOP
D I G E S T
— of —
DESPOTS
& DICTATORS

An A–Z of Tyranny

Text by GILBERT ALTER-GILBERT
Illustrated by STEVE KRAKOW

SKYHORSE PUBLISHING

Skyhorse Publishing books may be purchased in bulk at special discounts for sales promotion, corporate gifts, fund-raising, or educational purposes. Special editions can also be created to specifications. For details, contact the Special Sales Department, Skyhorse Publishing, 307 West 36th Street, 11th Floor, New York, NY 10018 or info@skyhorsepublishing.com.

Skyhorse® and Skyhorse Publishing® are registered trademarks of Skyhorse Publishing, Inc.®, a Delaware corporation.

Visit our website at www.skyhorsepublishing.com.

10 9 8 7 6 5 4 3 2 1

Library of Congress Cataloging-in-Publication Data is available on file.

ISBN: 978-1-61608-830-9

Printed in India

TABLE OF CONTENTS

D

E

F

G

S

T

TINPOTS

In the present day, the idea of dictatorship has assumed aspects of the comic opera, and conjures images of plotting generals and bulging Swiss bank accounts, but there is no denying the ongoing reality. The disease of dictatorship continues to ulcerate societies around the world from Asia and Africa to the Caribbean and the Middle East, and there remains no shortage of predators ready to carry forward the banner of brute absolutism.

The tragic pageant of despotism is inseparable from the shocking story of systematized and institutionalized torture and execution, purges, pogroms, genocide and ethnic cleansing. *Homo sapiens* has always excelled at devising fiendishly ingenious methods of oppressing his brother, and the catalog of atrocities attending the history of man's inhumanity to man is truly pornographic in nature. The reader should beware that the tyrant's cavalcade of crimes crosses from the ugly to the obscene: Only recently in Iraq, a survivor of Saddam Hussein's torture chambers had both his arms amputated joint by joint, starting with his fingers; another Iraqi refugee tells of watching his cousin receive an enema until his intestines exploded; in Iran, a Christian missionary was blinded by Moslem zealots who tied him to a table, spread honey on his eyes, then placed ants on his face; a torture victim of the last military dictatorship in Argentina was forced to watch as his 15-year-old sister was brutally raped by an 80-strong company of soldiers until she went insane—he himself was emasculated by his torturers with an acetylene torch.

The sad fact is that perpetual poverty, starvation, human slavery, international narcotics trade, routine life expectancy of thirty years, absence or denial of human rights, misuse of public funds, martial law, infant mortality, slums, famine, and disease, are ways of life in many countries—conditions which, traditionally, have afforded fertile ground for the growth of dictatorship, or which have been fostered by dictatorship already in place. Honduras, the original "banana republic," used to be run by a man who started life as a bus station timekeeper and, by the mid-1970s, the nation had more than 120 presidential changes since it declared independence from Spain in 1821; some African nations—Benin, for example, and Ghana, where people are said to care more about banana beer than politics, wallow in extremes of human misery so pathetic that they almost seem a particularly tasteless joke, but laughter quickly stops in the face of sewers choked with corpses, prisoners frogmarched to rendezvous with burial ditches among hundreds of acres of marijuana plants ten feet tall, peasants tortured with drinks of horse urine, and similar instances of sheer ferocity and unbridled cruelty. In the modern "national security state," the populace may be oppressed with more refined and "scientific" methods, such as brainwashing, punitive psychiatry, and harsh suppression of all dissent. Whether under the guise of "progress" or merely for his own perverted pleasure, whether by means of coup, putsch, junta, or tampered ballot box, whether with hammer and sickle or fasces and lictor, the despot, in his crazed vanity and quest for power, is more than willing to mete the most toxic pains and penalties to those who stand in his way. From Basil the Squint-Eyed to William the Silent and from Bismarck and Metternich to Bhaktiar and Bani Sadr, there have always been those who, like Suleiman the Magnificent, were only too eager to "take over the Standard, Mantle and Sword of the Prophet." In one form or another, the sultans and satraps, boyars and beys, nizams and nabobs, shoguns and shahs, rajahs and pashas, caliphs and viziers, grandees and margraves, emirs and hetmen, lieges and suzerains, kaisers and tzars, mikados and lords paramount are with us still, and their dynasties continue to flourish and prosper.

How is mankind to wrest free from the iron grip of this odious disease?

The answer is written on the wind . . .

A

SANI ABACHA (1943-1998) NIGERIA

Abacha's regime gave rise to the term "lootocracy" after his wife was caught leaving the country with 38 suitcases filled with cash (in addition to the stolen hundreds of millions in secret foreign bank accounts). Widely tied to allegations of corruption and human rights abuses, General Sani Abacha was responsible for hanging a number of anti-government activists, and for charging many others with treason. A military man since cadethood, he would eventually surround himself with a 3,000-man special guard while purging broader elements of the armed forces. He rigidly controlled the press as increasing international condemnation of his government rendered him a political pariah, and scoffed at sanctions threatened against him because of Nigeria's position as a significant supplier of petroleum to world markets. Abacha died suddenly at his presidential compound in Abuja. He was found in the company of several teenaged prostitutes. Some have speculated that Abacha's female companions may have slipped him a lethal Mickey. It is certain, however, that the Abacha clan deftly managed to lighten the national treasury by as much as $5 billion by plundering the money from the Central Bank then laundering it in offshore accounts. Since the demise of Sani Abacha, his name has been frequently invoked in the now-infamous Nigerian fee fraud scheme, where an e-mail is dispatched to unwary parties claiming to be a distress call from a family member of a wealthy African potentate now temporarily embarrassed by lack of funds, then asking for financial assistance with a promise of repayment and a generous bonus once the purported relative of the purported potentate has been restored to normal circumstances.

IGNATIUS KUTU ACHEAMPONG (1931-1979) GHANA

Ruled the African nation of Ghana from 1972 to 1978, before being deposed in a junta and executed by firing squad. Among the significant achievements of his regime were a reversal of highway conventions from left-hand driving to right-hand driving ("Operation Keep Right") and the upgrading of rickety sports stadia to international safety standards.

African kleptocrats who have salted away misappropriated funds in foreign banks and other business enterprises have been tagged "briefcase bandits." Egypt's Hosni Mubarak is reported to have plundered $40 billion; Sudan's Omar al-Bashir has hoarded $7 billion; and Nigeria's Sani Abacha, whose family the Swiss Supreme Court has declared a "criminal enterprise," has managed to stash $5 billion.

ALEXANDER THE GREAT (356 BC-323 BC) GREECE

After subduing the known world, famously wept because he had "but one world to conquer."

ILHAM ALIYEV (1961-) AZERBAIJAN

Since taking presidential office in 2003, Ilham Aliyev, son of presidential predecessor Heydar Aliyev, has given every indication of his intention to perpetuate a dictatorial dynasty in the newly established state of Azerbaijan, having set in motion all the usual dominoes: fake elections, crackdowns on opposition, establishment of one-party rule, disposal of term limits, and jailing of critics.

> Hung Hsu-Chwan was the leader of the Taiping rebellion that cost the lives of 50,000,000 people (yes, 50 million!).

IDI AMIN (1925-2003) UGANDA

A savage African thug who liked to refer to himself as "Field Marshall and President-for-Life Doctor Idi Amin Dada," he saw to it that, before they died, men, women, and children of whom he disapproved were horribly mutilated and tortured. A foreign service officer had his eyes gouged out, his genitals cut off, and was partially skinned before his body was dumped; some were run over by tanks at the military barracks; one nurse has told how she was ordered to decapitate six bodies and spray the heads with preservatives so they could be taken to Amin for his fun. He ordered the dismembered corpse of his ex-wife to be sewn back together, wheeled out of the mortuary, and shown to her three children. Amin's method of corpse disposal was for his "spooks" to bundle bodies into the trunks of cars and throw them into the river, where the crocodiles were supposed to eat them. A full-time boatman fished out the puffed and bloated corpses the crocs hadn't gotten to so they wouldn't jam the filter grids and water inlets on the hydroelectric generators at Owen Falls Dam outside Kampala; Amin stated that human flesh is saltier than leopard meat. His agents used methods like the sledgehammer routine, in which one prisoner is promised a reprieve if he batters his fellow to death; the same promise is made to a third man about him, and so on. In Amin's "State Research Bureau" and "Public Safety Unit," or internment and torture facilities, 500,000 were killed.

Idi Amin

ANNA (1693-1740) RUSSIA

Punished a trio of nobles by ordering them to impersonate hens. For each of the three, a large basket was shaped into a nest, padded with straw, and lined with newly laid eggs; the baskets were arrayed in a ballroom, and the offenders were costumed in feathers and directed, on pain of death, to squat on the nests and brood and cluck. Displeased with her relative Prince Michael, Anna commanded him to marry a notoriously ugly old scullery maid. Michael then was subjected to the most humiliating wedding celebrations ever devised: Empress Anna had ordered a magnificent public procession comprised of drunkards, cripples, deformed persons, derelicts, and freaks, followed by a parade of carriages pulled by pigs, dogs, and goats while the newlyweds took up the rear in a cage mounted on a shambling nag of an elephant. This farmyard fiasco concluded when the fantastic entourage reached the banks of the frozen river at the city's edge. As a wedding gift, Empress Anna had constructed an enchanting ice palace: The honeymooners' boudoir had been completed to the last detail and included an elegant four-poster bed, mattress, and pillows, all sculpted from ice, and accented by festively glacial decorations. Guards were posted at the doors so they couldn't leave.

OSWALDO LÓPEZ ARELLANO (1921-2010) HONDURAS

Honduran strongman who, in 1969, led his forces into battle against next-door El Salvador in the brief and bloody "Football War" triggered by a referee's decision at a soccer match. He lost. In 1975, the U.S. Securities and Exchange Commission discovered that the United Brands Company had offered a $2½ million bribe to President López if he would agree to reduce banana export tariffs. As a result of the ensuing uproar, trading of United Brands stock was halted and López was ousted in a military coup. This scandal is known in Honduras as "Bananagate."

The courtiers of homosexual King William II of England worshipped the pagan god Pan.

HAFEZ AL-ASSAD (1930-2000) SYRIA

Murdered 700 inmates at Tadmur Prison in 1980. In 1982, his troops turned their artillery on Hama, Syria's fifth largest city, to flush out some Muslim fundamentalists, killing 20,000 Syrian civilians. Syrian jails hold thousands of political prisoners. Assad's son, an opthamalogist by training, has assumed his father's rule, and continues to wage a violent and systematic war of repression against a rebellious populace frantic for freedom.

KEMAL ATATURK (1881-1938) TURKEY

Turkish parliament has instituted a law banning "insults to the reminiscence of" former ruler Kemal Ataturk and forbidding "destruction of objects" representing him. A special government website has been created to denounce other websites that defy this ban. So revered is Ataturk in his homeland that violations are punishable by the Turkish Minister of Justice rather than by a mere lower court prosecutor.

Juan Carlos Ongania was a 1970s Argentine dictator whose curious notion of orthotic cultural policy was to order a summary proscription of all manifestations of "immoralismo": long hair as a men's fashion, miniskirts, and avant-garde arts.

ATTILA THE HUN (406-453) CENTRAL EUROPE

With his original base of operations in present-day Poland, Attila the Hun was known as the "Scourge of God." His rampaging hordes reveled in indiscriminate slaughter, rape, looting, burning, unrestrained pillage, vicious diplomatic deceit, and other crimes. Such was their fiendishness that, in their day, popular belief held that Huns were the offspring of devils fornicating with humans. Huns inspired terror wherever they went; massacre, patricide, fratricide, infanticide, and incest were their stock in trade. Attila wielded the "Sword of Mars," a weapon found in a field and regarded as a gift from the gods—a sign that he was to rule the world. With it, he sacked over seventy cities in one year.

Attila the Hun

AURANGZEB (1618-1707) INDIA

Abul Muzaffar Muhy-ud-Din Muhammadr Aurangzeb, whose honorary title *Almagir*—or "World Dominator"—indicated his penchant for expanding the reach of his realm, was the sixth Mogul emperor, with a reign that lasted for half a century. His ambition to occupy the Peacock Throne drove him to fratricide; his aims as an evangelist for Islam drove him to similar excesses. A puritanical Moslem fanatic, he executed persons who refused to convert, outlawed music, and proscribed portraiture on the basis that viewing it amounts to idolatry—all while ruling over a quarter of the world's population.

> Elizabeth, Empress of Russia, owned 15,000 dresses and 1,000 pairs of shoes; she changed her outfit six times a day, and never wore the same dress twice. Among her army of lovers were courtiers, palace guards, gardeners, butlers, and soldiers.

ABDUL AZIZ (1830-1876) TURKEY

Ottoman sultan—on taking the throne, he ordered an eight-foot bed built and increased his harem to 900 women. His staff included 400 musicians who carried a dozen pianos to serenade him wherever he went. He had 400 grooms, 200 men to care for his private zoo, and

> Genghis Khan made war upon and destroyed the Empire of Persia because, contrary to his habit, the Persian monarchs wore their moustaches curling upward.

Abdul Aziz

5,000 additional servants. Among these was one man whose sole job was to replace the royal backgammon board after each use and another whose task was to sit around waiting for Abdul's fingernails to grow long enough for him to cut them. "He bought shiny new locomotives despite the fact that his country had no rails to run them on." For evening entertainment, the sultan ordered his troops to engage in mortal combat in the palace catacombs while he watched through a grate. "He chased chickens through the corridors of the palace until he caught one, then, as the captured hen fluttered frantically in the royal grasp, he would giggle and hang the Ottoman Empire's most prestigious award for gallantry around its scrawny neck." He bought expensive ships, but Turkey had no sailors. His orgies lasted four or five days at a time, then the royal scouts were dispatched to scour the land for new bedmates. Aziz called himself "Emperor and Conqueror of the Earth, Overlord of Emperors for All Time, and He Who Invests Monarchs With Their Crowns."

MOHAMED OULD ABDEL AZIZ (1956-) MAURITANIA

Coupmaster General Mohamed Ould Abdel Aziz used his position as commander of the Presidential Security Battalion to organize two different coups against Mauritanian heads of state. After playing a decisive role in defeating two additional coups attempted by rivals, he carried out a coup of his own, which propelled him to high position in the resulting regime. As this game of high-stakes musical chairs continued, he found himself dismissed by the beneficiary of the latest coup, and responded by deposing him and hijacking the helm of the national government. He then legitimized his power by orchestrating a phony election in which he temporarily stepped down from his position as military dictator and de facto ruler so as to be legally elected to the office of the presidency. During the period prior to his "election," Abdel Aziz had a hand in an ethnic cleansing episode in which 70,000 black Africans were expelled from Mauritania.

Mohamed Ould Abdel Aziz

B

IBRAHIM BABANGIDA (1941-) NIGERIA

Convivial and ever-smiling military dictator who ruled Nigeria with a rod of iron and dubbed himself the "evil genius." He once defused a coup in progress by disarming the ringleader with his bare hands; he would brook no opposition and went so far as to execute his closest friends if they dared to criticize him. His name became proverbial for fiscal malpractice: He is blamed for depreciating the value of Nigeria's currency through gross economic negligence and for misappropriating billions of dollars in oil revenues generated during the Gulf War. Babangida institutionalized corruption. He awarded fat contracts to foreign business interests and arranged embarrassingly bloated deals with his compatriots, prompting one commentator to observe, "If God were a Nigerian, Babangida would have attempted to bribe him."

JOAQUIN BALAGUER (1906-2002) DOMINICAN REPUBLIC

Joaquin Antonio Balaguer had been a trusted adjutant of Rafael Trujillo, the legendary Dominican dictator known as "The Goat." Proof of the value that Trujillo placed on the relationship is the "fact that Trujillo notoriously enjoyed humiliating and insulting his 'servants' in public, but never tried to degrade Balaguer nor to play practical jokes on him." Balaguer, in turn, served "El Jefe" faithfully, long-suffering and unperturbed by the dark and disturbing aspects of Trujillo's regime. In the chaos of the period immediately following Trujillo's death, Balaguer rose to power and clamped down on civil unrest. After serenading his constituents with a brief honeymoon of promised reforms, he restored the national course to business as usual, jailing opponents, shutting down newspapers, and killing intransigents.

The most stringent measure he adopted sprang from his love of trees. He outlawed commercial logging and closed the country's sawmills. The timber industry reacted by removing their operations from plain view, hiding them deep in the forests, and running their machinery at night. The situation called for drastic action and Balaguer, declaring logging to be a threat to national security, assigned the military to enforce the logging ban. The tense standoff reached a violent climax when a nocturnal raid on a clandestine logging camp turned into a gun battle that left a dozen loggers dead. The "war of the forests" continued for years. To mark the 500th anniversary of the arrival of Christopher Columbus in the New World, and a visit by the Pope, Balaguer launched a massive urban renewal program in the capital city of Santo Domingo and undertook construction of a colossal, ten-story lighthouse intended to project an illuminated beam in the shape of a Christian cross hundreds of feet into the night sky. The light from this $200 million structure, which is alleged to house the mortal remains of Captain Columbus, is supposed to be visible for many miles but has seldom been switched on, owing to frequent power outages and high energy costs. In 1994 Balaguer decided to run again for the presidency, although he was almost 90 years old and completely blind. The ensuing election was rigged in Balaguer's favor, and the fraud was exposed, with the result that the country was shut down by a general strike. At the age of 93, Balaguer tried one last time, seeking an eighth and "final" term as president. He lost and died two years later.

HASTINGS BANDA (1898-1997) MALAWI

In 1965, Hastings Kamuzu Banda proclaimed Malawi a republic with himself as president. He consolidated power and later declared Malawi a one party state. That one party, the Malawi Congress Party, then made him the party's President for Life and, the following year, he became President for Life of Malawi itself. He had returned to Africa from overseas in the shadow of a scandal: After completing his medical studies in England and establishing a practice in Scotland, he was caught in an affair with his receptionist, whom he had impregnated and left in the throes of a predicament which precipitated an ugly divorce. He drew attention in the 1980s when he banned radio stations from playing the Simon and Garfunkel song *Cecilia*. This was because, at the time, he was going through a rough patch with his mistress, also named Cecilia, and couldn't stand the conciliatory tone and attitude of capitulation implied by the song's lyrics. Banda was a lifelong bachelor, and kept Cecilia as a live-in companion and official hostess. Under Banda's stewardship, Malawi didn't have television until the 1990s. In his thirty-three years of rule, he never appointed a vice-president. His usual garb consisted of a three-piece suit, a homburg hat, a cane, and his sartorial signature, a flywhisk. With an enormous personal fortune and unlimited funds at his disposal, he built for himself an elaborate, 300-room palace, the centerpiece of a private compound that included a school and a grocery store. He was highly educated, yet sufficiently unconventional to indulge in such eccentricities as surrounding himself with bevies of female dancers who broke into spontaneous rejoicing at his approach. Anyone who rubbed him wrong was severely dealt with. In one incident, after three cabinet ministers and a member of parliament suggested to him that he implement certain reforms, they were killed the next day in a staged automobile accident the was announced to the press as the official cause of death, although it was later discovered that they had died as a result of having had tent pins hammered into their skulls. It was ordered that their caskets be kept closed and that they be buried at night. Adults were required to belong to the official political party. Membership cards had to be carried at all times, subject to random inspection. These compulsory cards were often bootlegged and sold by Banda's cadet corps, the Malawi Young Pioneers (MYP). Identification cards were so essential that there were instances in which they were sold to the yet-to-be-born. Banda used the Malawi Young Pioneers to monitor and intimidate the citizenry. The Pioneers had military training and were thoroughly indoctrinated in the tenets of "Kamuzuism." They carried weapons and operated a network of confederates and spies engaged in a program of domestic espionage. They served as Banda's personal bodyguards and circulated amongst the general populace in the capacity of enforcers, spreading a relentless climate of fear. Banda's presence was all-pervasive. It was against the law to hang a picture or a clock higher than the state-issued portrait of Banda adorning public buildings. An official dress code sanctioned by Banda specified parameters of grooming and apparel and compliance was demanded under threat of imprisonment. Even foreign visitors had to conform: Violators were designated "prohibited immigrants" and deported. Women were not permitted to wear trousers or skirts or dresses with hemlines above the calf. Men were forbidden to wear long hair or beards. "Flared pantlegs" were also forbidden for men. Infraction could result in a beating or an involuntary shave and haircut. Cinemagoers were treated to a stock propaganda film glorifying Banda prior to the presentation of the main feature. Kissing was not allowed in public nor were scenes in movies that displayed kissing. Movies, books and magazines were censored by the state. Phones were tapped and mail was opened. Television was nonexistent. Banda's censors screened news magazines for his personal use and ripped out any pages that might upset him or give offense. History pre-dating the Banda era was ignored or denied. Banda was unable to speak his native tongue, which necessitated a full-time translator—this function was carried out by his trusted security aide. Detractors were not tolerated. The slightest hint of criticism, even at the highest levels of his government, was met with instant retribution. Banda nursed an unrealized dream of building a new national capital city on the site of his birthplace. At the time of his death he claimed his age was 101.

"Valley of the Fallen"—what Omar Torrijos of Panama called Miami, referring to it as a place of final refuge for ousted dictators.

OMAR HASSAN AHMAD AL-BASHIR (1944-) SUDAN

Sudan's President Omar Hassan Ahmad al-Bashir has the dubious distinction of being the first sitting president to be accused of genocide by the International Criminal Court. Also accusing him of having embezzled $9 billion in state funds, the court has issued a warrant for al-Bashir's arrest. The warrant indicts him on five counts of crimes against humanity (murder, extermination, forcible transfer, torture, and rape) and two counts of war crimes (pillaging and intentionally directing attacks against civilians). Al-Bashir's government has also been accused of harassing investigators and of withholding information and tampering with evidence, as by concealing the location of mass graves containing his victims. Al-Bashir has reacted by announcing that his presidential jetliner will have a fighter escort at all times to prevent his apprehension abroad. The International Criminal Court has retaliated with a statement listing a fresh set of charges against al-Bashir including, in three separate counts, "genocide by killing, genocide by causing serious bodily or mental harm and genocide by deliberately inflicting on each target group conditions of life calculated to bring about the group's physical destruction."

BASIL II (958-1025) BYZANTIUM

Basil Bulgaroctonus, Emperor of Byzantium, who divided 14,000 prisoners into groups of 100, of which he blinded 99 and put out one eye of the remaining one, so that each Cyclops in each group of 100 could lead the other defeated enemies back to their homeland.

FULGENCIO BATISTA (1901-1973) CUBA

After serving as an elected president of Cuba from 1940 to 1944, Batista retired to live in the United States, then returned to the island nation in

Basil II

1952 to lead a coup by which he seized control of the country, suspended the constitution, and revoked political rights. He presided over an economy that favored affluent, entrenched business interests while disregarding general economic growth. Through collusion with American mafia interests, he established profitable deals in gambling, prostitution, and drug smuggling enterprises. As his administration became increasingly repressive—quelling dissent, imposing censorship of the press, and deploying secret police to contain opposition—he imprisoned large numbers of citizens while doing away with an estimated 20,000 more. Targeted by a successful revolution spearheaded by dictator-to-be Fidel Castro, he fled Cuba for nearby Dominican Republic, where he was afforded sanctuary by his friend and fellow tyrant, Rafael Trujillo. Eventually, he found refuge in Portugal, always keeping one step ahead of hit men dispatched by Castro to kill him. He died in Spain.

Fulgencio Batista

> Catherine the Great of Russia dropped the corpses of thirty-four thousand defeated Turks into the Danube through holes in the ice.

ANTONIO GUZMAN BLANCO (1829-1899) VENEZUELA

An opportunistic, Machiavellian caudillo who suppressed or supported the Catholic Church and other institutions as it suited his moods and interests. He filled the land with pictures and statues of himself. He advanced national progress while amassing a personal fortune and, although progressive in outlook and policies, could be brutally repressive when necessary, thereby setting a pattern that would be emulated by a long line of notable dictatorial successors including Cipriano Castro, Joaquin Crespo, and Marcos Perez Jimenez.

JEAN-BIDEL BOKASSA (1921-1996) CENTRAL AFRICAN REPUBLIC

A colonial veteran of the French army, where he eventually reached the rank of sergeant, Bokassa seized control of the Central African Republic, and promoted himself to the rank of Field Marshal, President for Life, Marshal of the Republic, and awarded himself so many medals and decorations that a special apron had to be sewn onto his tunic to accommodate them. Central African Republic is ravaged with diseases such as river blindness, bilharzias, and virulent gonorrhoeae. Men can expect to live to thirty-three, women to thirty-six. "Papa Bok," as his people called him, soon conceived the outlandish notion of converting the Central African Republic into the Central African *Empire*, with him at its helm; the cost of his ensuing imperial coronation would amount to a sizeable portion of the annual economy of the already bankrupt country. The emperor

21

would ride in a gilded carriage drawn by eight white horses along the capital city's (Bangui) only two miles of paved road; indeed, the plan was eagerly put into action and preparations got underway. For weeks prior to the coronation Bokassa pushed a model of the imperial coach up and down his palace floor, saying "me, me, me, me..." The great event took place after he had imported from France 150 tons of wines and cognacs, 400 tons of handcrafted furniture, thirty-five gray Normandy horses (life expectancy in the climate four to five weeks), the imperial crown (studded with 8,000 diamonds, topped by a solid gold globe of the world and valued at millions), the imperial throne (a massive, tasteless, three-ton monster shaped like an eagle), and four full-sized concrete replicas of the Arc de Triomphe. The imperial guard had uniforms tailored by Pierre Cardin, dignitaries traveled in sixty Mercedes limousines accompanied by 200 BMW motorcycles, and the natives were ordered to break into "spontaneous rejoicing"; the next day he appeared dressed as an eighteenth century admiral to review a mixed march—past of 200,000 citizens—a bizarre medley of pygmies, bare-breasted native female dancers, combat-clad assault troops equipped with Soviet weapons, musicians playing four-foot-long treebark trumpets, and American-style drum majorettes with white Busby hats. The coronation went along with all the panoply of crowns and ermine robes in the sweltering African heat, and the guests were treated to a magnificent banquet: Uniformed servants brought guests elaborately prepared delicacies which were, in fact, made from the flesh of a dozen prisoners Bokassa had recently fattened up before having them expertly butchered and served up to the unsuspecting guests, including foreign dignitaries, in this cannibal feast. On Mother's Day, 1971, Bokassa released all women prisoners but ordered the summary execution of all men convicted of assaults on women. One of the 48 medals he wore on his chest was nothing more than the badge of a Swiss ski resort. He planted a statue of himself at every crossroad in the capital. He swept the beggars from the city for his coronation. His crown alone cost 4% of the gross national product. Bokassa arrested and imprisoned two hundred schoolchildren when they protested that they couldn't af-

Jean-Bidel Bokassa

ford the uniforms he insisted they buy and wear; he then systematically beat them to death with his cane. When news of this incident reached the outside world, it provoked a military coup backed by France. Overnight, French Foreign Legion paratroopers stormed the presidential palace to discover a drained swimming pool containing the skeletons of thirty-seven more children, whose bones had been picked clean by Bokassa's pet crocodiles, lounging poolside; the half-eaten remains of another dozen bodies were found in the cold storage rooms of the kitchens; Bokassa was brought to trial for cannibalism, according to the indictment against him. He was charged with anthropophagy and with procuring corpses for the purpose of anthropohagy; with clubbing to death schoolchildren; with poisoning his two-day-old grandson; and with assassinating dozens of his advisors—the catalog of his atrocities went on and on...

> To express their contempt for the Brazilian "economic miracle" and the national slogan "Security and Development," citizens peed on the statues of heroes in the public parks.

C

CALIGULA (12-41) ROME

Deranged and treacherous Emperor of Rome. Caligula's horse Incitatus lived in a marble bedroom decorated with elegant classical paintings. Caligula gave the horse birthday parties and promoted Incitatus from senatorial rank to Consul of the Roman Empire. To raise revenue, he prostituted his sisters and the wives and daughters of senators and nobles. He ordered his army to line the beaches at Boulogne and massed troops there and placed catapults and archers facing the ocean, then he waded into the water with his unsheathed sword to lead a frontal assault against the god Neptune who had offended him by wrecking some of his ships. Archers fired their arrows, and infantry slashed at the surf, stabbing the seawater with their spears and swords. Caligula had a lifelong incestuous relationship with his sister, declared himself a god, and built a temple where he worshipped *himself.*

CARACALLA (188-217) ROME

Roman emperor whose real name was Marcus Aurelius Antoninus, but who assumed the nickname he was given because of the Gallic tunic he often wore. An intriguer from an early age, he orchestrated the undoing of his father-in-law by circulating false reports, and murdered his brother and all his followers so that he wouldn't have to share the throne. Becoming unhinged, Caracalla next embarked on a binge of indiscriminate homicide, racking up 20,000 kills in the total tally, including the entire male population of one city where he locked the unfortunate victims in a gymnasium before dispatching them. Eventually, Caracalla was stabbed to death by an assassin of his own guard while stopping on a country road to relieve himself under a tree.

FIDEL CASTRO (1926-) CUBA

Communist revolutionary embodying the summit of hypocrisy: After "liberating" his homeland from the grip of right-wing dictator Fulgencio Batista, Castro quickly installed himself as a left-wing dictator in a charade that lasted fifty years. Nicknamed "The Beard" in homage to the sprawling bush of chin-fringe that accents the military fatigues, khaki cap, and fat Cuban cigars that are his trademarks. A windbag of gargantuan proportions, he is given to rambling, ten-hour speeches fueled by drugs and ridiculous ideological posturings of his own invention. He keeps Ernest Hemingway's rotting fishing yacht, *Pilar,* languishing alongside a ramshackle dock because he's too cheap to repair it. He has spent millions in an effort to export his brand of revolution around the globe, while subjecting his own people to cultural stagnation and dire privation. The destitution and political oppression which prevail in Cuba have driven many to acts of desperation such as absconding by night in dilapidated boats plying shark-infested waters in a bid to escape (no one is allowed to leave voluntarily). In recent years, Castro has relinquished the reins of power to his brother Raoul so lucky Cubans can continue to enjoy the many blessings of life in a nation that is operated as a private fiefdom. *Viva Fidel!*

Fidel Castro

> Modern Brazilian police departments have patented several new brands of torture, including the "parrot's perch," the "dragon chair," and the "pianola Boilenson."

CATHERINE THE GREAT (1729-1796) RUSSIA

Russian tzarina of German ancestry. Assigned herself the title "The Mother of the Fatherland." Married off at the age of fifteen to a Grand Duke (later Tzar Peter II) described as "twisted and deformed with an ugly, thick-lipped face, who behaved like a whimpering child one minute and a drunken sadist the next." She could barely bring herself to sleep with him but found, somewhat to her relief, that he was impotent and spent bedtime either blind drunk or playing with his toy soldiers; eight years after the nuptials, she remained a virgin. After his assassination, which she contrived, she inherited the throne and began to make up for lost time with a succession of lovers that is legendary: Serge Saltyakov, Count Poniatowsky, Gregory Orlov, whom she presented with the Nadir Shah, or Orlov diamond, as a bauble, and Prince Potemkin, each more handsome and dashing than the next. She conceived a mania for beautiful young men, whom she had appraised, graded, and brought to her bedchambers for an exchange of favors. These romps in the boudoir became the ramp to wealth and position for many a young stud, be he soldier, statesman, or stable boy. She excelled at court intrigue and at deceitful diplomacy, legal chicanery, and blackmail. She waged appalling wars of aggression and occupation which expanded her empire from Poland to the Crimea and the Black Sea. She "treated her wretched serfs as scarcely human." She maintained a correspondence with the leading figures of the

Catherine the Great

Enlightenment—Montesquieu, Diderot, Voltaire and Grimm—while she institutionalized at a state level the deplorable condition of the serfs who comprised fifty percent of the population, worked from sunup to sundown, and lived from cradle to grave in abject servility. This feudalistic system of exploitation was entrenched and flagrant: Serfs were valued less than dogs or livestock and those rejected as worthless by landowners were placed in the servitude of the state as "economy peasants." She ordered the murder of her own son, so that he could not constitute a threat to her claim to the throne. After decades of dalliances with increasingly youthful toyboys, bloody Catherine, guilty of uxoricide and infanticide, and of the deaths of thousands in battle in foreign lands, and the miserable subjugation of millions at home, expired of a stroke while sitting on the toilet.

NICOLAE CEAUSESCU (1918-1989) ROMANIA

Following his downfall, a torture table in the makeshift morgue of one of his "interrogation" chambers was sworn by rattled guards to be haunted by the screams of departed victims. Ceausescu had the world's largest collection of pornographic films, including home movies of himself and his three children participating in sex orgies, a West German paper reported.

Nicolae Ceausescu

CHARLEMAGNE (742-814) FRANCE

When holding court, he demanded that visitors and ambassadors alike fall on their knees and kiss his feet. Illiterate, he commissioned councils and conventions to interpret theological issues according to his wishes. He kept a harem comprised of women from all his conquered lands and that included his sister. He forced conquered peoples to accept Christianity at swordpoint; those who refused were mowed down, as happened when the sanguinary monarch shattered the column of Irmin sacred to the Saxons and decapitated 4,500 of those he held captive when they didn't immediately accept conversion. In his relentless quest to spread the faith, he enthralled all of Europe in a wave of pomp, persecution, and servitude.

Charlemagne

> Mariano Melgarejo, dictator of Bolivia, was a drunkard who turned the presidential palace into a brothel for orgies.

CHARLES V (1500-1558) SPAIN

Perpetrator of the sack of Rome, during which the city was put to the torch by vandalist German troops during what came to be known as the "German Fury." As the city burned, thousands of bodies lay in the gutters, and the pope was held in a dungeon by the invaders. Charles was as greedy and ambitious at heart as he was stunted in stature; described as a "little man, sickly, rheumatic, and arthritic, son of a lunatic woman and a worthless playboy, possessed by the idea of being the first to rule the whole world; a world that had already thrown the reins of a hundred countries into the feeble hands of this broken body with its shifty mind."

KHORLOOGIIN CHOIBALSAN (1895-1952) MONGOLIA

In the 1930s, made himself the subject of a personality cult patterned after that of his hero, Josef Stalin, whose predilection for lethal purges Choibalsan emulated by corralling tens of thousands of those perceived as ideological nonconformists or threats to the state, and imprisoning them in penal colonies; he killed as many as 100,000, including close to 20,000 Bhuddist monks, whose temples he demolished by the hundreds, even though he had himself, as a youth, prepared for priesthood.

CLAUDIUS (10 BC-54 AD) ROME

Roman emperor who was unlucky in love. One of his wives, the nymphomaniac Messalina, slept with half the male population of Rome, even going so far as to sneak out of the imperial palace in disguise at night and hire herself out as a prostitute in local bordellos. After her death, Claudius prevailed on his Praetorian Guard to kill him if he ever again attempted to marry; later, however, he betrothed his half-unhinged niece Agrippina, sister of Caligula, whose fidelity was even flimsier than Messalina's. The day of her wedding to Claudius, he executed dozens of senators and hundreds of knights who objected to the union; soon thereafter, Claudius was poisoned to death by none other than this same blushing bride.

CLEOPATRA (69 BC–30 BC) EGYPT

The Queen of the Nile is reputed to have performed fellatio on 100 visiting centurions during the course of a single evening; introducing several novel sexual practices to the pride of the Roman army; when she ran out of Romans, she resorted to a basket of asps.

Cleopatra

CLOVIS (466-511) FRANCE

Assassinated all the princes of the Merovingian family, subdued the Thuringians, and, using Christian conversion as a pretext, waged constant war against his "heretic" neighbors, the Burgundians and Visigoths.

CHANG HSIEN-CHUNG (1606-1647) WESTERN CHINA

Bloodiest butcher of the ages who killed more than 40,000,000 people in 5 years including 32,300 students, 27,000 Buddhist priests, 280 of his own wives, 400,000 women accompanying his army, 600,000 inhabitants of Chengtu, and 38,000,000 inhabitants of Szechuan, where he destroyed every building in the country. Chang pronounced himself emperor of the Daxi Dynasty. When scholars rebuked his claim, he slaughtered them en masse. Next, he ploughed through the women, merchants, and all the officials. Then he commanded his soldiers to kill each other and to cut off the feet of the officers' wives and stack them in a pile. Chang was obsessed with ears and feet and instructed his guards to collect the ears and feet of all those killed in outlying areas so that he could tally the number of victims. When he had finished his rampage, he erected a stele bearing the inscription:

Heaven brings forth innumerable things to help man
Man has nothing with which to recompense Heaven.
Kill. Kill. Kill. Kill. Kill. Kill. Kill.

In one area devastated by Chang, the population dropped from 3,102,073 to 18,090; in another area, the number of inhabitants was reduced from 400,000 to 20.

Huns, Vandals, Goths, and other barbarians led by despotic warlords skinned victims to make coats, sawed off the tops of their skulls to make cups, and drank their blood. As raiders, they reveled in appalling carnage, and their prowess for maiming and mutilating was matched by their relish for plundering, pillaging, and amassing booty.

COMMODUS (161-192) ROME

Called himself "The Emperor Caesar Lucius Aelius Aurelius Commodus Augustus Pius Felix Sarmaticus Germanicus Maximus Brittanicus, Pacifier of the whole Earth, Invincible, the Roman Hercules, Pontifex Maximus, Holder of the Tribunician Authority for the Eighteenth Time and Father of the Country," and who wanted to rename the Eternal City "Commodiana." He fancied himself a gladiator—in which capacity, in fact, he excelled. He was strangled to death by a wrestler.

CONSTANTINE (288-337) ROME

Enterprising pagan who, in a supreme act of political cynicism, embraced Chrisitianity and used it as a banner under which to unify and gain ascendancy over the disintegrating Roman Empire. After forming a nominal alliance with an early pope, he sidelined and overrode the papacy, and strongarmed all subjects under his jurisidiction into conformity with the true faith; any who failed to accept Christianity wholeheartedly were declared heretics and eradicated in droves. Under Constantine, "all temples and academies, all statues and structures, all works of art and literature that were not immediately and directly appropriated by the Catholic Church were obliterated from the face of the earth." Constantine expunged his wife and son and his rival Licinius, along with countless other threats to his rule or to his comfort and complacency. He waged wars of conquest and oppression and shifted the seat of Roman power to the city of Byzantium, which he renamed Constantinople in honor of himself, and there established a strong, centralized government that twentieth-century dictator Benito Mussolini took as a model for his own totalitarian system.

D

PORFIRIO DIAZ (1830-1915) MEXICO

Sporting a walrus moustache, a plumed hat, a tasselled sash and sword, and enough medals on his chest to anchor a battleship, Porfirio Diaz exuded an avuncular air that belied his appearance. Serving a total of eight terms in office, Diaz governed Mexico for a total of thirty-five years, during a period known as the Porfiriate. Ironically, he had begun his political career based on a platform with the slogan "No re-election!" He was known for other felicitous mottoes regarding his policies and beliefs and what could be expected of him. Examples include: "Little of politics and much administration" and "bread or a beating," meaning "take what you're offered and be grateul or face the consequences." Perhaps his most resonant utterance was the order he gave to a provincial governor instructing him how to deal with a group of rebels: "Kill them on sight!"

DIOCLETIAN (245-313) ROME

The "Scourge of the Tiber." His reward to himself after a lifetime spent assiduously persecuting Christians was the resplendent Temple of Jupiter, a grandiose mausoleum set aside as his final resting place.

Trujillo of the Dominican Republic cruised the streets of Santo Domingo, and Bokassa of the Central African Republic cruised the streets of Bangui, on the prowl for underage girls.

SAMUEL DOE (1951-1990) LIBERIA

Following a month of rice riots in 1980, Liberia's Samuel Doe led a military coup, slaying President William R. Tolbert, Jr. in the Executive Mansion. Many of Tolbert's supporters also died in the fighting. Cabinet members were publicly executed and government ministers were paraded naked through the streets of the capital city, Monrovia, before being summarily executed by a firing squad on a nearby beach. Hundreds of government workers fled the country, while others were imprisoned. Doe's vendetta continued unabated in a steady drum roll of ongoing executions, cutting down scores of Tolbert's functionaries, who were refused both legal representation and trial by jury. Charles Taylor, a former ally of Doe's, slipped into Liberia from Côte d'Ivoire in late 1989 to launch an assault against Doe. Taylor had broken out of a jail in the United States, where he was awaiting extradition to Liberia under indictment for embezzlement. By mid-1990 most of Liberia was controlled by rebel factions. Doe was captured by rebels and tortured before being killed. The spectacle was videotaped and seen on news broadcasts around the world. Viewers watched captors slurping beer as Doe's ear was sliced off.

DOMITIAN (51-96) ROME

A handsome youth, his sexual orientation was ambivalent although he tilted towards a preference for men. As soon as he had been named as Caesar, he undertook a vicious purge of the senate. He was extremely cruel, and veritably ingenius in devising sadistic methods of torture and execution, many of them nothing short of obscene; he was astute, as well, in his use of psychological torments. His profligate and decadent reign was abruptly ended when an assassin drove a knife into his groin, and his accomplices chopped the body to pieces. His body was hacked into so many bits that his wife had them stitched together so that a sculptor would have a model from which to chisel a commemorative statue.

JEAN-CLAUDE DUVALIER (1951-)

Upon Francois Duvalier's death, his chubby, baby-faced son Jean-Claude assumed the mantle of power. "Baby Doc," as Jean-Claude was generally called, was heralded by government propaganda as the "Bright Lighthouse of the Nation" but was known popularly as the "Fatly Inflated Tire" and "Furniture-Face, the Appointed Son." After taking up where his father left off and, through liberal application of the dreaded Macoutes, maintaining order in the AIDS-riddled, shockingly impoverished island nation, all the while pilfering the national treasury at every opportunity and selling body parts of deceased citizens, Baby Doc finally met his reckoning when the fed up and infuriated Haitian people turned against him in earnest. Rioters with rocks and clubs hunted down the Tontons and cornered them one by one. While one Tonton had his clothes ripped away from his body in the street, another drew his pistol and shot himself from guilt and fear of retribution. Seventy-five Tontons were killed by the enraged mobs in the first day of upheaval. Baby Doc and his wife Michelle arranged for asylum in France and boarded the first plane out, where they took up cozy residence in Grenoble, and proceeded to lead the lavish lifestyle of idle plutocrats. When, in 2011, after fifteen years of exile in France, Baby Doc unexpectedly showed up at the Haitian capital's airport in Port-au-Prince, he was promptly arrested.

E

GNASSINGBE EYADEMA (1937-2005) TOGO

President of Togo from 1967 until his death in 2005. He participated in two successful military coups, became President after the second, and emerged victorious in three uncontested elections. Assassination attempts plagued his presidency. He was the sole survivor of a plane crash in the northern region of Togo where he later built a lavish memorial at the site of the accident. Following another attempt on his life by a bodyguard, he wore the extracted bullet as an amulet. In a subsequent incident, an army base where he was staying was assaulted, and several people, including his chief of staff, were killed, yet Eyadema himself escaped unharmed. When he appeared in public, a retinue of 1,000 dancing girls accompanied him, singing his praises as he passed. Special edition wristwatches were fitted with dials that flashed his portrait at fifteen-second intervals and comic books presented him as an invincible being with superhuman strength. The date of the plane crash from which he alone had walked away was officially remembered each year as the Triumphant Celebration of the Defeat of Evil. Eyadema didn't meet his end in the fateful plane crash but, during a medical emergency, as he was hurriedly being evacuated to the nearest hospital, he died on an airplane, after all.

> Maharajah Mulhar Rao, Gaekwar of Baroda—executed criminals by having them stepped on by an elephant.

F

FAROUK I (1920-1965) EGYPT

Lecher, gourmandizer, reckless driver, and a kleptomaniac (he stole Winston Churchill's pocket watch) and self-indulgent, self-gratifying sensualist par excellence. He liked carbonated beverages and especially favored orange soda, which he drank by the gallon. He kept a library of pornography. After suffering nightmares about lions, he took his rifle to the Cairo Zoo and shot the beasts in their cages. He had his large fleet of automobiles painted bright red and made it a crime for anyone else to own a car this same color, so that police would not stop him when he used the highways as his personal speedway. If anyone tried to overtake him, he shot at their tires. He was such a wild driver that government officials ordered ambulances to follow whenever he took to the road so they could pick up the innocent casualties; A warehouse was commissioned to store the objects (watches, wallets, lighters, powder compacts) he had pick-pocketed at parties. In his forties, he grew incredibly lazy and spent his days in a shuttered room gorging on chocolate bonbons and watching television. Gluttonous and grossly obese Farouk liked nothing better than to crawl under the table of a fancy restaurant to suck the toes of his 18-year-old girlfriend Irma Minutolo, a former Miss Naples. At a restaurant one evening, while in the company of another young Italian beauty, he died at age 45 after devouring a dinner of raw shellfish, lobster thermidor, a triple portion of lamb, haricots verts, assorted desserts, and a serving of fruit.

FRANCISCO FRANCO (1892-1975) SPAIN

Prim, old-fashioned, and stodgy, Spanish genralissimo Francisco Franco couldn't help but be a monarchist and a defender of the Church. He found his passion, however, when it came to slaughtering his countrymen. Representing the traditionalist nationalist faction in a vicious civil war during the late 1930s, Franco was assisted in his efforts to massacre hundreds of thousands of his countrymen by weapons, troops, and aircraft supplied by Italy's Mussolini and Germany's Hitler; in the aftermath of the strife, having emerged victorious, he enlisted the aid of a quasi-fascist paramilitary organization called the *Falange*, or Phalanx, whose members were picturesquely attired in black jackboots and quaint, glisteningly shellacked three-cornered hats, to wage a ruthless campaign to hunt down and systematically exterminate any remaining opposition in a bloody reign of terror. Franco maintained his authority over Spain for another three decades, curbing the freedom of the press, crushing dissent, and keeping the populace firmly under his thumb. The glories of his exploits are symbolized by the vast burial complex at The Valley of the Fallen. Conceived and built by him using lottery funds, Franco envisoned this stately memorial garden as a place of tribute designed to honor the victims of the Spanish Civil War. Following his death in 1975, Franco was interred in the basilica built into the base of a cliff, whose façade comprises the dramatic backdrop for a hilltop cross and adjoining grounds, Tellingly, Franco spurned the idea of burial there, desiring Madrid as a locale, instead.

Francisco Franco

Persian Shah Agha Mohammed Khan put out the eyes of 20,000 citizens of Kerman when they refused to bow down to him.

G

GALBA (3 BC-69 AD) ROME

Son of a hunchback, Servius Sulpicius Galba had a lifelong sexual predilection for markedly older men and, as Emperor of Rome, it was a curious preference he could well afford to indulge. He had ample opportunity but before he could run though more than a handful of elderly toyboys, he was caught in the toils of the constantly broiling soap opera that was the game of the imperial succession, and he was murdered and replaced on the throne by the ever-scheming Otho, protégé of one of his former lovers.

ERNESTO GEISEL (1908-1996) BRAZIL

A sort of dictator lite, Ernesto Beckmann Geisel faithfully represented Brazil's military and other socio-politically conservative elements in defending the nation and its hallowed traditions by dutifully torturing or murdering anti-establishment radicals while hushing the press, then quietly retiring from the presidency to run a private chemical company.

Haile Selassie—Ethiopian Emperor worshipped as a divinity in the Jamaican Rastafarian movement.

GHENGIS KHAN (1162-1227) MONGOLIA

While still a youth, killed his brother in a quarrel over a fish. He slaughtered every man, woman, and child in a tribe of nomads that had dared to kidnap his wife. Defenders were put to the sword. A resisting governor had molten lead poured into his eyes and ears. Khan wiped out a Shah's army of

Ghengis Khan

400,000 in a day. Women were raped in front of their families. Surviving civilians were herded by the tens of thousands into living shields at the front of Genghis' armies as he attacked each new objective and cut it to ribbons. Each was gashed open after Genghis discovered that one old woman had swallowed some pearls. His savagery was shocking, and he thought nothing of slaughtering hundreds of thousands of innocent civilians as he went. Severed heads of residents were arranged in three gruesome pyramids of men, women, and children. The "mightiest and most bloodthirsty conqueror of all time" was a machine of extermination, laying gory waste to everything in his path; in another incident, in one morning, 70,000 Magyar warriors were massacred, so that the roads for two days' journey from the battlefield were strewn with corpses as the rest tried to flee.

JUAN VICENTE GOMEZ (1864–1933) VENEZUELA

An indigene from the mountains of Venezuela, Gomez began life inauspiciously as a barely literate cowboy living on a ranch in the Andes region. In manhood, he rapidly grew in stature, exchanging the role of a regional strongman for the occupancy of the presidential palace. Never married, he sired close to 100 children. He was called "The Catfish" on account of the resemblance of the stringy tips of his moustache to the barbels of the aforementioned aquatic animal. He ran Venezuela as a personal playpen; suspending congress and adopting extraconstitutional powers, he built up the country and made a fortune in the process. A fierce chieftan who ruled with an iron fist, he kept rivals and enemies in a perpetual state of fear. There were spontaneous outbreaks of jubilation in the streets upon the announcement of his death.

> General Pinochet of Chile referred to his regime as an "authoritarian democracy"!

LEOPOLDO GALTIERI (1926-2003) ARGENTINA

One of the chief architects of Argentina's "Dirty War," during which 30,000 political undesirables were "disappeared" by being drugged and hurled alive from airplanes into the ocean and rivers or buried in unmarked graves. A member of the junta that spawned Argentina's last dictatorship—the so-called "National Reorganization Process"—Galtieri had personal jurisdiction over a death squad known as Intelligence Battalion 601, which reported directly to him. During the National Reorganization Process, labor unions and political parties unions were outlawed along with internal regional governments, and the economy floundered as a campaign of systematic civil repression was carried out against Argentine citizenry. Thousands of individuals branded as subversives mysteriously vanished, becoming *desaparecidos*, or missing persons. Galtieri's government grew increasingly unpopular until he hit on the idea of claiming sovereignty over the Falkland Islands, a British territorial possession lying off Argentina's coast. In hopes of improving his political fortunes, Galtieri ordered a military invasion of the Falklands, which provoked an unanticipated military response from the British Navy. In the resulting armed conflict, the British retook the islands and so embarrassed the proud Argentine military that Galtieri's entire government came crashing down. Alcoholic Galtieri was summarily removed from office, charged with human rights violations and mismanagement of the Falklands War, and was condemned to be stripped of rank and placed before a firing squad. These terms were commuted and he received a twelve year prison sentence, instead. Ultimately, the charges of human rights abuses which had been filed against him were dropped, but he was found guilty of bumbling the war and, for this, he was sentenced to a term of imprisonment. Before he could serve his time, he was granted a presidential pardon.

British police advisors refused to work in Iran under the Shah, whose prisons they called "toenail factories" because all that came out of them was "toenails and screams."

H

HISSENE HABRÉ (1942-) CHAD

During Hissene Habré's eight-year reign in Chad, from 1982 to 1990, human rights abuses were rampant. Habré maintained a dreaded political police force known as the DDS (Documentation and Security Directorate) whose agents extracted information under torture and practiced whole-sale liquidation of dissidents. Among DDS interrogation techniques were application of chemical sprays into the nose, mouth, and eyes; waterboard-ing; scalding and burning with incandescent instruments; forced ingestion of fluids, and fitting the mouths of detainees around fuming automobile exhaust pipes. It has been calculated that the number of Chadians killed at the hands of the DDS falls in the neighborhood of 40,000 while more than 200,000 were subjected to detention, interrogation, and torture. In addition to these atrocities, Habré mounted ethnic cleansing pogroms targeting such groups as the Hadjerai, the Zaghawa, the Sara, and oth-ers, arbitrarily netting them in mass arrests whenever he considered them a threat. In 1990, a rebel offensive soundly defeated Habré's forces and soon thereafter entered the Chadian capital of N'Jamena. The dictator took flight, exiting through Cameroon, then finding refuge in Senegal. In March, 2006, the European Parliament demanded that Senegal turn over Habré to an international court in Belgium. Senegal did not comply. Two years later, a Chadian court sentenced Habré to death *in absentia* for war crimes and crimes against humanity.

ABDUL HAMID II (1842-1918) OTTOMAN EMPIRE

Also known as "Abdul the Damned," Hamid was a paranoid Ottoman sultan (successor to Abdul Aziz) who wore armor under his robe and a lead-lined fez; all his food and drink was tasted before he would touch

it, and his garments were tested before they were worn so as to be sure
they hadn't been laced with poison. His water supplies were defended
by sentries. Any cow or goat providing him milk had a twenty-four
hour guard and his documents were purified by heat and disinfected
before being presented to him. He built himself a palace that was a
cavernous, booby-trapped vault. With an unscalable wall on one flank
and the ocean on the other, the palace complex involved more than a
hundred buildings fronted by deceptive facades and partitions designed
to mislead and confuse. Palace agents combed every corner of this laby-
rinth, patrolling night and day. Inside, Hamid regularly switched his
living quarters and the furniture was arranged so visitors could enter
only in single file. Many rooms were connected by secret passages;
others featured cupboards containing pistols which would fire auto-
matically if disturbed. The sultan's food was prepared in kitchens with
locked and bolted windows and doors. If he suspected a fork or spoon
had been contaminated, he would demand to be fed by hand by one of
his harem girls. He was so paranoid about possible plots that he built
an entire village designed only for his safety. Behind the barricades he
kept loaded pistols in every room—two hung beside his bath—and constructed glass cabinets which, when opened, blasted the rooms with bullets from remote-controlled guns. He personally shot dead a gardener
and a slave girl whose sudden movements alarmed him.

JAMES A. HARDEN-HICKEY (1854-1898) TRINIDAD

James Aloysius Harden-Hickey, Esquire was born in San Francisco,
the scion of a wealthy Irish miner and a French mother of aristocratic
descent. He proudly traced his lineage to Norman nobility and the
Spanish king Milesius. He was schooled in France on the fringes of
the court of Napoleon III. He married a French countess and, in
1878, was made a baron of the Catholic Church. After the collapse
of Napoleon III and the reinstatement of the Republic, he edited, in
Paris, a reactionary royalist newspaper called *Le Triboulet*, named after

the jester of Louis XII. His activities in connection with this journal resulted in forty-two lawsuits, heavy fines for his staff, his fighting of at least a dozen duels (he was an expert in the use of arms), and his temporary expulsion from France. After the newspaper disintegrated, he exiled himself to England, where he rejected Catholicism and embraced Thesosophy. He undertook a trip around the world. A storm at sea drove his ship aground on a deserted volcanic island seven hundred miles off the coast of southern Brazil—a bleak, mistenshrouded, lava-encrusted spot called Trinidad. He studied Sanskrit and spent a year in India at the feet of holy men, after which he made brief excursions to China and Japan. He returned to Paris where, having divorced his first wife, he met and married American heiress Anna Flagler, daughter of financier-philanthropist John Flagler, iron and oil tycoon, and early developer of the state of Florida. He took up residence in the Flagler family mansion in New York, where he occupied himself translating a book on Buddhism, completing the volume *Bible Plagiarisms*, concocting schemes whereby to convert Americans to Buddhism, and composing eleven novels, a literary encyclopedia, and his masterpiece: *Euthanasia: the Aesthetics of Suicide*, a two-hundred-page meditation on the virtues of self-annihilation. Meanwhile, he took advantage of a loophole in international maritime law, which allowed any party to take possession of uninhabited territory not claimed by a sovereign power. Remembering the barren cliffs and rocky ravines of the sixty-square-mile volcanic outcropping where he had once been marooned in the mid-Atlantic, he crowned himself James I of Trinidad, and claimed the island for his own. With promises of buried pirate treasure, and plans to mine the plentiful deposits of guano, Harden-Hickey hired an army of coolies to do the manual labor, and tried to lure settlers to his new-found "kingdom." He opened a chancellory, and printed his own bonds and currency. He offered his own postage stamps, and issued medals and decorations. Then, in 1895, the British navy seized the little island for use as a coaling station. Immediately Brazil claimed sovereignty. Pathetically, the frustrated Trinidadian

Adolf Hitler

resulted in his arrest. Sentenced to prison, he wrote his memoris—*Mein Kampf (My Struggle)*—which set forth his philosophy and documented his travails. To put his theories in practice, he ignited the Second World War, which ultimately wiped away 70,000,000 persons. As leader of the Nazi Party, Hitler envisioned the advent of a 1,000 year reign of a utopian, globally dominant greater German state he called the Third Reich. Populating this utopia would be a Master Race comprised of specimens of pure Aryan bloodlines whose insulation from contamination was imperative. With this rationale, Hitler orchestrated a systematic genocide of Jews, gypsies, homosexuals, mental defectives, and other "social undesirables." Antisemitism on a colossal scale was manifest in the Final Solution—the total extermination of the Jewish race. Nazis regarded Jews as human vermin—confined in urban "ghettoes" where they were starved to death or herded onto trains which deported them to vast concentration camps, they were conscripted to do forced labor or were killed in gas chambers disguised as bathing or de-lousing facilities. Gold was salvaged from the teeth of their corpses. Others were subjected to gruesome, bizarre, and inhuman medical experiments, extending to vivisection without benefit of anaesthetic. Still others were simply removed to locations where they were made to stand or kneel at the edge of large trenches before being shot. In all, 6,000,000 met this fate at the hands of Hitler's SS, an elite corps charged with the mission of solving the "Jewish Problem." When Allied forces reached the concentration camps at the war's end, they found thousands of emaciated bodies piled in mass graves which their tormentors hadn't had time to bury; in other cases, they reached camps in time to liberate walking skeletons, so wasted from malnutrition they barely had skin enough to cover their bones. Hitler's colorful henchmen included a failed novelist, a former chicken farmer and drug addict, and an occultist. Under the sign of the swastika, Hitler invaded and subjugated all of Europe until repeating the mistake made by Napoleon and ending up crippled by the Russian winter. Hitler's stormtroopers had effectively implemented *blitzkrieg* (lightning war) to overrun most of the continent and his brilliant scientists had engineered advanced technology such as long-range rockets and other terrifying new weapons, but these advantages came too late, and Germany's enemies inexorably began to close in on the capital of Berlin. As the end approached and he hid in an underground bunker, Hitler's personal physician kept him going with strychnine injections and other stimulants. Adolf Hitler committed suicide in his fuhrerbunker and his body was burned per his request. During the war, Hitler's agents confiscated priceless artwork and other resources from all over Europe; some of it has never been recovered.

HONG XIUQUAN (1814-1864) CHINA

Hong Xiuquan, whose honorary name was Huoxiu, was a Chinese prophet and revolutionary who led the Taiping Rebellion or "Rebellion of Great Peace" against the Qing Dynasty, establishing the Taiping Heavenly Kingdom over portions of southern China and ruling over 30 million people, with himself as the "Heavenly King" and self-proclaimed brother of Jesus Christ. The conflict between Hong's army of "God Worshippers" and the forces of the Qing apparatus aided by the French and British resulted in a death toll of between 20 and 30 million, due both to warfare and starvation. Hong's militaristic, theocratic regime, preaching a peculiar form of Christianity, introduced reforms such as the rejection of Confucianism, abolition of foot binding, communal property ownership, and separation of the sexes, although Hong himself kept a covey of concubines. As a young man, having completed his studies at a school called Book Chamber House, Hong headed off to take civil service examinations and, along the way, heard a Christian missionary preaching about the religion. A year later, he failed the examinations and suffered a nervous collapse. During his recovery he experienced mystical visions in which a man in a black dragon robe with a long golden beard gave him a sword and a magic seal, and told him to purify China of demons. After this episode, friends and family said he became authoritative and solemn. Seven years later, he began to examine the religious tracts he had received, and was

Hong Xiuquan

soon converted. Hong burned all Confucian and Buddhist statues and books he had at home, and began to preach to his community about his visions. His first converts were relatives of his who had also failed their examinations. Together they set out on a spree of idol demolition in hamlets and small villages, rousing the indignation of Confucian citizens and officials who regarded them sacrilegious. As a symbolic gesture to purge China of Confucianism, Hong commissioned two giant swords called the "demon-slaying swords" to be forged. By 1850 Hong had between 10,000 and 30,000 followers. Authorities were alarmed at the size of the rapidly multiplying sect. The imperial troops of the Green Standard Army were sent against them and ordered them to disperse. When they refused, a battle ensued and, although his enemies outnumbered him ten to one, Hong emerged the victor. He slew a deputy magistrate, decapitated the Manchu commander, and proclaimed the establishment of the "Heavenly Kingdom of Transcendent Peace." Hong Xiuquan ruled his kingdom by issuing frequent edicts from his Heavenly Palace, demanding strict compliance with Hongian moral tenets. When Yang Xiuqing, an ambitious comrade in arms and fellow Heavenly Kingdom Taiping leader, formed a network of spies and began claiming to speak directly with God, Hong grew suspicious and had Yang and his family liquidated. Hong died from poisoning, ostensibly a suicide some said was from eating manna—a command from the Bible he had given his people as they starved.

Benito Mussolini outlawed publication of photos or drawings of skinny women in Italian newspapers, ads, and government publications under threat of jail.

ENVER HOXHA (1908-1985) ALBANIA

Like all despots, Albania's Enver Hoxha was the embodiment of ego. He built enormous, architecturally distinctive monuments to himself, decorated the landscape with statues of himself, emblazoned mountainsides with his name, and published sixty-five books extolling the universal wisdom of his thoughts. A passage conveying an inspiring snippet of Hoxhaism prefaced every schoolbook used by Albanian children. Deep-seated paranoia caused him to pepper the Albanian landscape with half a million defensive concrete bunkers intended to foil invasion by any external enemy while a high-voltage electric fence encircled the country to prevent entry or, more especially, exit. If the fence did not stop an infiltrator or escapee, minefields and booby traps would. Dissemination of all information to the populace was strictly controlled by state media. A secret police force called the Sigurimi was so effective that, as a result of its monitoring activities, one out of every three Albanians had at one time or another been investigated by its agents or served a sentence in a labor camp. The slightest utterance of complaint against Hoxha's regime could result in accuations of treason or "disruption of the proletarian dictatorship," followed by imprisonment or execution. Purges of such "traitors" occurred regularly and could extend to the highest-ranking members of government. Show trials were commonplace and the kangaroo courts in which they were conducted emphasized their verdicts by arresting or ostracizing relatives of defendants and accusing them of complicity in "crimes against the people." Sigurimi detainees could expect questionings, beatings, physical and psychological torture, and solitary confinement merely as a prelude to more serious persecutions. Hoxha maintained six penal institutions specifically designated for political prisoners and fourteen labor camps. Attempts to "escape outside the state" or refusal to return by those allowed to travel temporarily on official business were punishable by death. A former tobacconist, Hoxha considered himself a genius whose seeds he bestowed on the citizenry by commenting on everything from economics to military affairs. His insights included encouraging a higher birthrate by rewarding prolific women with a *Heroic Mother* certificate and condemning beards as contrary to hygiene. Because of his dazzling leadership, the government accorded him such honorary appellations as *Great Teacher, Sole Force Ultimate Comrade*, and *National Savior*. A museum would be consecrated to his memory as a showplace for the wonders of Hoxhaism and the glories of his reign. A fitting tribute to the isolationist *par excellence* who "turned Albania into a hermit state and suffocated an entire society to the point of lifelessness."

HUANG-TI SHIH (259 BC-210 BC) CHINA

Emperor who inaugurated the construction of the first of the million steps of the Great Wall of China and built an immense canal linking China from north to south. Huang unified China by banishing the divergent philosophies and moral guidelines that characterized the so-called Hundred Schools of Thought and brought far flung regions into conformity under a single code of obedience to his law. Huang handed down an edict calling for most books of the time to be burned, on the grounds that they contained no useful information. Owning forbidden books was punished severely: Hundreds of scholars were burned alive for this offense. Huang busied himself with new construction projects, including gargantuan palaces, and erected the Twelve Bronze Colossi, which were made from captured weapons that had been melted down. As he advanced in years, Huang grew increasingly apprehensive about the approach of death, and he embarked on a desperate quest for the fabled elixir of life, which would supposedly grant him immortality. He was obsessed with acquiring it and fell prey to many who claimed to possess it. He sent an emissary to the island of Zhifu in search of a mystical mountain where a thousand-year-old magician was rumored to have his abode. Huang hoped that the magician could aid in his quest. He sought out alchemists and supernaturalists and anyone demonstrating abilities that might allow a man to live forever. Since

Huang-ti Shih

the emperor was fearful of evil spirits, he annexed to his two hundred palaces a network of tunnels and subterranean passageways so that he could evade interaction with evil spirits by traveling unseen. When a meteorite crashed near the Yellow River, someone embellished it with an inscription prophesizing the death of the emperor. When Huang heard about this, he sent an ambassador to investigate. As no one confessed to the deed, everyone in the vicinity was put to the sword. The stone was then scorched with fire and ground to dust. Soon thereafter, while making an inspection of the eastern provinces, the emperor died as a result of swallowing mercury pills intended to render him immortal. Huang's chief advisor worried that news of the emperor's demise could trigger a massive uprising and, since it would take two months' travel time to reach the capitol and stabilize the realm, such an uprising could not be prevented. It was decided, therefore, to conceal the emperor's death for the remainder of the journey. Only a handful of those in the emperor's entourage knew about the death; most were kept ignorant. As it was summertime and the imperial caravan had to contend with the seasonal heat, the chief advisor instructed servants to place carts loaded with rotten fish behind and ahead of the imperial wagon; this way, the smell of the fish would mask any telltale odors which might emanate from the emperor's decomposing flesh. The Recording Historian reports that "they pulled down the shade so no one could see his face, changed his clothes daily, brought food and when he had to have important conversations they would act as if he wanted to send them a message."

VICTORIANO HUERTA (1850-1916) MEXICO

The installation of mild-mannered Francisco Madero as president of Mexico at the climax of a bitterly fought but victorious revolution was cause for rejoicing among the masses of the country's poor and oppressed. But the "Christlike" Madero, as bandit-turned-freedom-fighter Pancho Villa characterized him, was anathema to the hacenderos—the mighty hereditary

Victoriano Huerta

landowners who were used to running Mexico as a feudal empire. They conspired with the commander of the federal army, General Victoriano Huerta, to overthrow Madero and regain the reigns of power. Contriving a pretext by which to arrest the "gentle liberator," Huerta staged a coup d'etat and assassinated Madero during an alleged escape attempt. With his black jackboots and riding gloves and menacing "coke bottle" glasses, Huerta looked every inch the villain. His first actions as dictator were to suspend the parliament and snuff out any opposition. During his term in office, eighty-four congressmen were jailed, and several others executed, along with a high-ranking judge who dared to criticize him. His counter-revolutionary policies immediately stirred up a hornet's nest and, within days of his having seized power, a fresh wave of indignant rebel armies were on the march to contest him. Eventually, his rule, which was rife with murder or incarceration of his opponents, and which earned him the nickname "The Jackal," became so distasteful to his neighbors to the north, that U. S. president Woodrow Wilson dispatched a fleet of warships to shell the port of Veracruz, disembarking squadrons of marines with the aim of pressing the coastal invasion inland to the presidential palace in the capital and apprehending Huerta. As pressure against him mounted, Huerta fled first to Jamaica, then to Europe, and then to the United States, where he was arrested and imprisoned in a military jail in El Paso, Texas. A chronic alcoholic who drank claret and brandy with breakfast, he died shortly after his release from detention, as a result of a severely cirrhosed liver. His legacy is the pattern of overpopulation and impoverishment that persists to the present day, thanks to the corruption and ineptitude of successive governments and the duplicity of Vatican doctrines.

SADDAM HUSSEIN (1937-2006) IRAQ

An obsessive compulsive paranoiac, Saddam Hussein washed his hands forty times a day, and took three to four showers a day, always in a different place. He had a team of six doctors do nothing but make special soaps, shampoos, toothpastes, and body creams for him; he was afraid of

Saddam Hussein

being poisoned by ordinary products. When he traveled he took along his own food which he had a bodyguard taste before he would touch it. He also took his own chair everywhere he went because he was afraid an assassin might place a poison-coated tack or needle in a seat cushion. In one of his first acts as leader, he executed twenty-one of his henchmen, so they couldn't overthrow him. One of Hussein's luxury bunkers was a $100 million underground fortress lavishly equipped with a heated swimming pool, tanning machines, fancy tiled bathrooms, stereo systems, TV sets, VCRs, washing machines, microwave ovens, and other modern conveniences. The completely air-conditioned 5,400 foot bunker had six-foot-thick walls, and was built to withstand a nuclear blast. A war room was equipped with chairs featuring seat belts to be used in the event of a bomb rocking the structure, which was also fitted with a sophisticated communications system and a television studio, and furnished with Italian antiques, French chandeliers, and water filtration and sewage systems.

> After the death of Evita, Argentine strongman Juan Peron consoled himself with a 14-year-old girl.

FELIX HOUPHOUET-BOIGNY (1905-1993) IVORY COAST

A descendant of wealthy chieftains and a trained physician, he spent his early professional years practicing medicine in rural areas. In 1990 he built, among coconut groves and tin shacks, the largest church in the world, a $200 million basilica with a dome higher and wider than St. Peter's in Rome, and donated the edifice to the Vatican (which accepted it), in a country with a Roman Catholic community of only ten percent of the population, and a foreign debt of $15 billion.

I

IBRAHIM THE MAD (1616-1648) OTTOMAN EMPIRE

Ottoman sultan whose body ballooned to a butterball at an early age. Often tipsy and careless in his dress, he drenched his beard, turban, clothes, and person with reeking perfumes. He had a fetish for fur, and shaved his pet cats so that they could be outfitted with sable coats. When he tired of having his harem girls frolic as fillies to his stallion, he cavorted with fat women; he had his entire harem thrown into the Bosporus when one member was caught as unfaithful.

IVAN THE TERRIBLE (1530-1584) RUSSIA

Russian Tzar Ivan's reputation was so shocking that, when a horrified young girl heard she'd been chosen as his third wife, she died of fright, and occupants of a castle besieged by Ivan chose to blow themselves up rather than fall into his hands. His auspicious beginnings found him, as a mere boy, amusing himself by hurling dogs and other small animals from the 200-foot-high towers of the Kremlin to their deaths on the pavements below. As a ripening juvenile delinquent of 14, he rode his horse through the streets at full tilt, indiscriminately killing and maiming hundreds of pedestrians. At the age of 16 he seized power from his boyar guardians, had 30 of them hanged, and declared himself tzar; protestors were beheaded, thrown to the dogs, or had their tongues cut out. Still a teen, he poured alcohol on some petitioners and set their hair on fire. In young adulthood, he banged his head against walls and floor, smashed furniture and furnishings, and pulled out the hair of his beard by the fistful. He carried a pike with which he gored those who annoyed him, and he loosed trained bears to attack innocent

Ivan the Terrible

Like Panama's Manuel Noriega, President Nagarta Tombalbaye of Chad summoned Haitian witch doctors and conducted Stone Age occult ceremonies in a desperate attempt to stay in power.

IEYASU TOKUGAWA (1543-1616) JAPAN

Last shogun of Japan; a brutally effective military leader, warlord Tokugawa unified disparate feuding clans under the umbrella of the shogunate and established the foundation for a centralized national government that would employ countless thousands of bureaucrats for generations to come. Jealous of his position, Tokugawa neutralized potential rivals without compunction. He entrenched himself in an impregnable fort and coordinated a political equation in which his family exerted exclusive dominion over the whole of Japan. Thus, a new nation was formed by the strength of his personality, but at the cost of absolute autarchy and an ethos of violence and ferocity. Tokugawa offered no alternative to his leadership and heads rolled at his slightest displeasure.

J

JAHANGIR (1569-1627) INDIA

Father of Shah Jahan, who built the Taj Mahal, Jahangir was an indolent mogul emperor with a weakness for opium and alcohol. He preferred to leave affairs of state to his scheming and ambitious wife. He squashed like bugs and swatted like flies those who dared distract him from his devotion to his pleasures and to the cultivation of the arts.

JUSTINIAN (482-565) ROME

Justinian's greatest claim to fame revolves around his storied romance with the magnificent whore Theodora, his partner both in the bedchamber and in the councils of state; less well known is the precedent he set for centuries of anti-semitism to follow: his *Corpus Juris Civilis* codified all the anti-Jewish laws from Hadrian to his day, and added a few discriminatory statutes of his own. Jews were not permitted to leave legacies; they were not permitted to build synagogues; and not permitted to recite prayer. Jews who denied the resurrection could be deprived of their property. Mass conversions under threat of execution were common under Justinian.

> Ayatollah Khomeini's autograph sells on the open market for twice the price of Winston Churchill's.

K

ISLOM KARIMOV (1938-) UZBEKISTAN

Islom Abduganiyevich Karimov, born an orphan in Samarkand, became First Secretary of the Communist Party of Uzbekistan and, in 1990, the country's first president. In the capitol of Tashkent, there are few foreign embassies and the Karimov regime extends its control over any semblance of private enterprise by means of a regulatory arm managing what it calls GONGOS, or Government Organized Non-Governmental Organizations. Karimov thwarts all political opposition, perpetuates his rule through shady electoral practices, and restricts all political activity by invoking a prerogative called the Law on Internal Debate. Under Karimov, universities are not allowed to teach any subject that relates to the critique of public issues. In one notorious incident, the government killed hundreds of protestors and has targeted certain religious groups for routine persecution. Imprisonment without trial, use of torture, and vanishings have been reported. Uzbek elections have been termed a "travesty" because of the absence of political choice. Under Karimov, the state maintains a censorship bureau and a State Inspectorate for the Protection of State Secrets. The state strictly controls the tone and subject matter of all publications and generously tolerates "approved criticism" while denying expression of "unregistered opinions." The tarnished record of Karimov's security apparatus includes a sordid litany of crimes by the police, including torture, kidnapping, murder, and rape, while financial corruption, religious persecution, and censorship remain the province of other agencies. An example of the regime's excesses is the case of two prisoners who were boiled alive in 2002.

A reenactment of the return of Ayatollah Khomeini to Iran from exile in France was staged by the Iranian military using three eleven-foot-tall cardboard likenesses of Khomeini devised by army personnel. One of the replicas was greeted as it emerged from a plane and was carried between rows of soldiers on dress parade so that Khomeini could "inspect" them. Soldiers stood at attention and saluted it as it passed. Another cardboard cutout was seated in a limousine for a reenactment of the return to the capital from the airport. A third cardboard Khomeini was stationed nearby so that it could watch the proceedings.

RUHOLLAH MUSAVI KHOMEINI (1900-1989) IRAN

Ayatollah Khomeini was hurled by the mob into the leadership of Iran after the fall of Shah Reza Pahlavi. He was an atavistic mullah who instituted, during the final decades of the twentieth century, a medieval Islamic theocracy. Under Khomeini's government by clergy, citizens were publicly flogged for drinking alcohol; bootlegging became a multimillion dollar trade. After 2,000 drug-related executions and the incarceration of 50,000 addicts in labor camps, official statistics put the number of addicts at one million. Khomeini's remains repose in an elaborately ornate tomb resembling a classical mosque.

Ruhollah Musavi Khomeini

KIM JONG-IL (1941-) NORTH KOREA

Sporting elevator shoes, a bouffant hairdo, and a belted jumpsuit, and bespectacled with oversized eyeglasses that wouldn't have looked out of place on the aging Elvis, the chubby Jong-il looked like an Asian Liberace found lounging at a Lawrence Welk Resort. He was behind a bombing that killed 17 South Korean officials, sank a South Korean naval ship without provocation, and ordered the downing of a Korean Air flight that killed 115. He was afraid of air travel himself, and would only travel by train. Once he rode in a 16-car private rail entourage all the way to Moscow; stations along the way were stocked with fresh lobster for consumption en route. He was a gourmand who is said to have had a personal wine cellar stocked with 10,000 bottles and a personal sushi chef who went everywhere with him. He had all-night banquets, some of which would last for four days. Second in a line of three dynastic dictators leading North Korea according to the principle of *Juche*, a political ideology of self-reliance which guides the peaceful, freedom-loving North Korean people in every thought and deed and which was incarnated in Jong-il's father Kim Il-sung, fondly described as "the ever-victorious iron-willed brilliant commander and outstanding military strategist brimming with Juche-based strategy and tactics and immortal feats performed in defeating US imperialism and defending the freedom and independence of the fatherland!," Kim Il-sung is supposed to have purchased 40,000 gold watches filigreed with portraits of himself and his son to give to loyal party members on the occasion of his sixty-fifth birthday. When it came time for junior to succeed him, Jong-il busied himself developing intercontinental missiles and a nuclear weapons program while huge numbers of his citizen comrades suffered destitution and starvation. He maintained dismal concentration camps characterized by the harshest conditions and turned North Korea into a hermit state, cutting it off all but entirely from contact with the outside world. Since the advent of Kim governance, North Korea has observed a policy of *songun*, or "military first"; North Korea boasts one of the largest standing armies on the planet, but cannot feed its own people without outside help. By invading South Korea, Kim Il-sung started the Korean War which cost two to three million lives and left the traumatized Korean Peninsula permanently divided. Belligerent, isolated, secretive, insular, crippled by chronic food shortages, North Korea suffered a famine in the 1990s that took a million lives. Nevertheless, the malnourished population had to forget its prolonged food deprivation long enough to come out in throngs to make public displays of adulation for the "Dear Leader" whenever summoned. According to the official version of the circumstances of Jong-il's death, he was on a train conducting field inspections when he succumbed to the rigors of "sitting up all night, having uncomfortable sleep, and taking rice-balls." A humble servant of the people, the "Dear Leader" had been on his way to dispense "field guidance" to the farmers, factory workers, and soldiers he regularly addressed, when he was overcome. While touring on a train which inexplicably carried four hospital cars, Jong-il "continued in common attire to carry out his painful labors despite the biting cold weather" and his "patriotic devotion blocked the howling wind of history till the last moments of his life." At the moment of his death the state news agency reported that a "natural wonder" occurred: "the skies glowed red above sacred Mount Paektu and the impenetrable sheet of ice at the heart of the mystical volcano cracked with a deafening roar." The ruptured ice and the "unprecedented loud crack" purportedly manifested at Chon Lake on sacred Mount Paektu, the site where the country claims Jong-il was born at the moment foretold by a swallow and heralded by a double rainbow, according to the official narrative. Then a huge snowstorm ensued, which itself immediately was followed by an illustrious sunrise which lit up the words carved into the mountainside, "Mt Paektu, holy mountain of revolution. Kim Jong-il." The funeral cortege of Lincoln limousines wound bleakly past the central square of the snowswept capital, Pyongyang, as women wept and serried ranks of soldiers in olive drab bowed their heads in homage along the same streets ordinarily buzzing with official sedans transporting party officials and frequently knocking down unwary pedestrians. In the face of the passing of the Dear Leader, whose life, according to Korean News Agency headlines, was "Bright as Snow" and inspires North Koreans to "Ardently Yearn for Kim Jong-il" and to "Make Uninterrupted Efforts to Build a Thriving Nation," succession has fallen to the son of the "Dear Leader" and grandson of the "Eternal President," Kim Jong-un, a twenty-seven-year-old four star general educated in Switzerland, whose name means "righteous cloud." The inauguration of the reign of Jong-un, already dubbed "The Great Successor," and hailed as the newest standard bearer for the code of Juche, offers little hope for the hundreds of thousands of North Koreans immured in labor camps, subjected to relentless hardship, torture, hunger, or execution. According to United Nations statistics, life expectancy for North Koreans is $3\frac{1}{2}$ years shorter than when "Eternal President" Kim Il-sung, the current leader's grandfather, expired eighteen years ago.

Kim Jong-il

GENERAL KRIANGSAK (1917-2003) THAILAND

General Kriangsak Chomanan was Thailand's prime minister from 1977 to 1980. In 1976, in what came to be known as the "Thammasat Massacre," police and paramilitary "Village Scouts" stormed the Thammasat University in the Thai capital of Bangkok and slaughtered students who were accused of insulting the crown prince. They butchered the students and abused their corpses in the streets. A military junta then seized power; a million books were burned; charity workers gathered 300 corpses; eight thousand were arrested as security threats to the state; and thousands of other protesters fled to the countryside. Soon afterward, partly in reaction to these events, military strongman Kriangsak Chomanan staged a successful *coup d'etat*, declared himself "National Peacekeeper," and took over as premier as well as minister of the Interior and Supreme Commander of the Armed Forces. During Kriangsak's regime, Bangkok was riddled with fleshpits and an estimated 300,000 prostitutes and 400,000 heroin addicts called the city home. Kriangsak reportedly permitted the People's Republic of China to ship arms to the Khmer Rouge in Cambodia in exchange for the withdrawal of Chinese support for communist insurgents in Thailand.

> Moammar Qadaffi's bloody button-down brown shirt and silver wedding ring were among the deceased dictator's personal effects offered for sale online after he was dragged out of a drain pipe, cap-captured, and killed by insurrectionists.

KHOSRU II (?-628) PERSIA

King of Persia who lived in such splendor that when he went on a journey, 1,000 slaves watered the roads before him and another 200 walked on ahead to scatter perfumes. Son of the monarch Khosru I, who fought the fabled Roman general Belisarius and perpetrated a cruel massacre of the Mazdakites, he was eventually murdered by his own son.

Menelik II—Ethiopia; died after swallowing the Bible's Book of Kings, in an attempt to cure himself after suffering a stroke.

L

VLADIMIR LENIN (1870-1924) RUSSIA

Robbed Russia of the legimitate democracy which followed tzarism and replaced it with the Bolshevik dictatorship of the Kremlin. He enlisted the services of Felix Dzerzhinsky—"Iron Felix"—as head of the Cheka (forerunner of the KGB) to deploy an army of commissars and operatives in long leather trench coats to spy on the populace as the tzar's OGPU had done before it. Lenin swore to rid the body politic of "parasites," and commenced to murder 300,000 fellow citizens in a wave of "Red Terror" that swept throughout the newborn nation and inaugurated a totalitarian bulwark that would breed untold misery for untold multitudes for the next seventy years. The carefully embalmed, hermetically encased body of this heroic personage rests in a glass-domed tomb at the foot of the Kremlin walls.

Vladimir Lenin

LEOPOLD II (1835-1909) BELGIUM

King of Belgium whose brutal policies in the colony of the Congo reduced its population of 20 million by half in a two decade period. Personifying imperialism at its worst, Leopold hired the famous explorer H. M. Stanley ("Dr. Livingstone, I presume?") to carve out treaties with Congolese chiefs in order to legitimize a massive land grab in central Africa. Next he declared all unoccupied territories and their resources property of the Belgian-controlled state, subjugating the entire native population to a life of forced labor on the rubber plantations. Floggings and amputations by machete were common methods of maintaining discipline among the work crews comprised by the indigenous populace. Punitive patrols were dispatched by the imperialist masters if rubber production quotas weren't met. Anti-exploitation literature including *Red Rubber* and *Congoland: A Story of Wrongdoing* heralded a storm of protest over Leopold's African policies and, under the pressure of international condemnation, Leopold annexed the Congo a year before his death.

Leopold II

Deposed dictator Idi Amin went to Saudi Arabia; Jean-Claude "Baby Doc" Duvalier went to France; Imelda Marcos went to Manhattan where, after being acquitted of absconding from the Phillipines with hundreds of millions of dollars, she threw a party in her penthouse for the jurors; Stroessner went to live in Brazil in a comfortable villa on a leafy lane; Nguyen Cao Ky of Vietnam went to Los Angeles, then to Dulac, Louisiana.

FRANCISCO SOLANO LÓPEZ (1827-1870) PARAGUAY

Paraguay's Francisco Solano López launched the War of the Triple Alliance against Argentina, Brazil, and Uruguay. In this war, Paraguay lost 9/10ths of its population. On charges of conspiracy and treason, he had 68,200 people put to death, including his two brothers, two sisters, two brothers-in-law, and his mother. Pampered as a child, Solano López was appointed to the rank of brigadier general at the age of eighteen. In his twenties, Solano traveled to Paris, where he became infatuated with the empire of Napoleon III and Napoleon himself. López equipped his army with exact copies of uniforms of the Napoleonic army. He ordered for himself an exact replica of Napoleon's crown. While in France, he met Parisian courtesan Eliza Lynch and brought her back with him to Paraguay. There she was his mistress and de-facto first lady till his death, strongly influencing his later ambitious schemes. Returning to Paraguay with large quantities of arms and military supplies, he became Minister of War in 1855 and next was appointed Vice President by his father. When the latter died in 1862, López called together a congress that unanimously chose him as president for ten years. He was an insatiable philanderer, and his wrath was implacacle when a woman dared to spurn him. Solano López consolidated his power after his father's death in 1862 by silencing several hundred critics and would-be reformers through imprisonment. Another Paraguayan congress then unanimously elected him president. "A monster without parallel," as one contemporary described him, Solano López's grotesque miscalculations and warped ambitions plunged Paraguay into a war that nearly erased the country from the map. Many "saw Solano López as a paranoid megalomaniac, a man who wanted to be the 'Napoleon of South America," willing to reduce his country to ruin and his countrymen to beggars in his vain quest for glory." Eliza Lynch survived her husband, lost her lands, buried her husband with her own hands after his defeat in the last battle in 1870, and died penniless some years later in Europe.

LOUIS XIV (1638-1715) FRANCE

Known as "The Sun King" because his presence was considered so brilliant that all the world revolved around him. The powdered and perfumed monarch dressed peasants in bird outfits, replete with colorful feathers, and used them for target practice. When nobles pointed out to him that he was bankrupting the state with his extravagant expenditures, he replied, "I am the state." At Versailles, the narcissistic royal built the most opulent palace Europe had ever seen where he held court and expected every noble in France to dance attendance. He mustered the terrifying dragonnades and dispatched them afield to feed his appetite for mercenary conquest, triggered wars in every direction, in pursuit of riches to replenish state coffers depleted by sardanapalian indulgence and he laid the groundwork for resentment and planted the seeds of indignation that would soon spell the end for his species as it contemplated in horror the rising tide of revolution.

Louis XIV

King Adahoozou I of Dahomey lined the walls of his capital with the heads of his subjects; when builders reported there weren't enough heads to finish the project, the king replied, "Get more or I'll use yours."

M

SAMORA MACHEL (1933-1986) MOZAMBIQUE

As soon as Marxist revolutionary Samora Machel settled into his role as Mozambique's first unelected president, his FRELIMO party annihilated any opposition to its rule. SNASP, the National Service for People's Security, and PIC, the Criminal Investigation Police, initiated a wave of arrests, filling both prominent prisons and "re-education camps" in remote locations. Machel's estranged wife was placed in detention although she refrained from all political activity. Citizens were under perpetual surveillance by roving teams of enforcement cells set up in residential neighborhoods and in the workplace. Suspected dissidents were rounded up and later expunged. Even fellow militants were arrested, under any convenient pretext. In one macabre incident, several of Samora's former cohorts were picked up and accused of treason. They were interned in a re-education camp and told they would be transferred to Maputo, the capitol, for trial. Somewhere along the way, at the side of a lonely road, the jeep in which they were riding came to a halt. The soldiers, using a mechanized excavator, had dug a trench in the road shoulder and dumped a load of lumber in the opening. The prisoners were trussed up with thongs, thrust into the trench, and drizzled with gasoline. Then the wood was set ablaze. The prisoners were roasted alive, while the soldiers circled the trench singing FRELIMO anthems.

FELIX MALLOUM (1932-2009) CHAD

Immediately prior to the term of Chadian overseer Felix Malloum the Sahel Drought brought with it disastrous effects including widespread famine and mass starvation, leaving scarred survivors stumbling in the sand with swollen bellies and toothpick-thin limbs, bereft of basic necessities such as water and medicines. Malloum was in prison where he had been incarcerated by President Nagarta Tombalbaye who summoned the aid of witch doctors and reenacted primitive occult rituals in a desperate bid to stay in power. Tombalbaye made his officials drink the blood of a tongue ripped from a live chicken and undergo ordeals like crawling through a termite nest, and imbibing foul concoctions to induce violent vomiting. Delusional, drinking round the clock, and hoarding his money in a cardboard box, he announced "the spirit of their ancestors" would speak to the Chadian people. Sure enough, the spirit spoke. "This is the voice of your ancestors. We have chosen Nagarta Tombalbaye to guide you to your destiny," the radio proclaimed. Within weeks, commandos stormed the palace and nabbed him. According to reports, "when he refused to surrender and board a lorry waiting to take him away, they cut him down in a spray of machine gun bursts." Malloum was released from prison to head the Supreme Military Council, which then ran the country. The constitution was scrapped and political parties outlawed. Civil war broke out and, just to complicate matters, neighboring dictator Moammar Qadaffi invaded and attempted to occupy a large area of land where rich uranium deposits were rumored to exist. With the assistance of the French Foreign Legion, Malloum managed to patrol and defend his northern border and expel the Libyan forces. Malloum put down an attempted coup and executed its ringleaders while striving to provide basic necessities in a country lacking even fundamental infrastructure such as wells and cattle feed. Eventually, Malloum retired from public life and relocated to Nigeria. He returned to the Chadian capitol N'Djamena in 2002, after twenty-three years abroad. Upon return he was entitled to the various benefits provided to former presidents: a monthly stipend, a residence, and coverage of all medical expenses, along with two vehicles and a driver.

MAO TSE-TUNG (1893-1976) PEOPLE'S REPUBLIC OF CHINA

Communist con man Mao Tse-tung uplifted the Chinese people by perfunctorily murdering them by the tens of millions. A fraud and a hypocrite, he betrayed every ally who trusted him, living regally while advising his countrymen to harness themselves to an ethos of humility, duty, and sacrifice. As uncontested leader of the People's Republic, his enlightened social policies included sending much of the population to re-education camps and herded like cattle to work, under gun and lash, on communal farms, while separating the elderly from their kin and relegating them to "Happy Homes" where they were "occupied with menial tasks such as rope twisting or mending and where they would soon perish, lonely, frustrated, hungry." For the benefit of the ignorant masses, Mao published his *Little Red Book*, filled with vapid prescriptions for leading an anti-bourgeois life. He sagely raided the national treasury to finance weapons programs and military buildups while starvation ravaged half the country.

Mao Tse-tung

FERDINAND MARCOS (1917-1989) PHILLIPINES

Marcos had a reputation as a Lothario; his most famous conquests were his wife Imelda, a former beauty queen with a passion for expensive shoes and the charming American b-movie actress Dovey Villagran. In 1972, ostensibly because of civil unrest and separatist guerilla activity in various locales among the 7,000-island Phillipine territorial chain, Marcos declared martial law, dissolved the legislature and placed 30,000 political opponents in detention. A favorite implement in his torture cells was the "cranker dynamo," a hand-cranked, battery-powered device featuring electrodes which were attached to toes, ears, and testicles. Marcos wore a bulletproof vest. He had homes in London and in Switzerland, and business interests all over the Philippines. Marcos personally controlled all business contracts arranged with foreign investors and owned Manila's major newspaper, the *Daily Express*. He devoted a great deal of his time to boosting a Free Trade Zone for industrial development, which happened to be situated on land he owned. Marcos encouraged foreign investment from multinational corporations by offering controlled labor unions and a minimum wage that was below the official subsistence level, according to the government's own statistics. During Marcos' tenure, Filipinos ate, per capita, fewer calories of nourishment each day than the people of India.

MENGISTU HAILE MARIAM (1937-) ETHIOPIA

Under the reign of Ethiopia's Mengistu bodies of murdered children were left in piles by the roadsides for the hyenas. Mengistu's death squad was called "The Stranglers." He had children jammed into trucks, ordered at gunpoint to dig their own graves, then machine-gunned by the assassination crews. Attaining power on the coattails of a junta led by a faction known as the Derg, Mengistu is alleged to have smothered Emperor Haile Selassie with a pillow to clear the path for Derg

100

ascension. Mengistu's African vampire state arrived at its zenith with the "Red Terror" campaign of genocide against anti-Derg factions— half a million persons purportedly died during this phase. As head of state, one of Mengistu's first acts was to nationalize property belonging to his own grandmother, a circumstance said to have infuriated her. Out of sheer spite, Mengistu executed a number of ministers and high-ranking military officers, including a commanding general who disliked Mengistu and told him, when he was a young officer, that he would "chew him like chewing gum" and spare him no amount of suffering. He warned his adversaries that he would soon "make these ignoramuses stoop and grind corn!" Many of Mengistu's victims were done in by the "Kebeles," the neighborhood watch committees which served as local level security surveillance units. Families had to pay the Kebeles a tax known as "the wasted bullet" to obtain the bodies of their loved ones. During the Ogaden War, when Mengistu heard that Ethiopian units were beginning to mutiny, Mengistu flew to the front and ordered mutineers bayoneted as "cowardly and counterrevolutionary elements." Mengistu's irresponsible policies contributed to a vast Ethiopian famine to which more than a million succumbed. Mengistu crushed a coup attempted against him 1989, but was overwhelmed by rebel forces in 1991 and fled to Zimbabwe, where he enjoys asylum as a guest of President Mugabe. In 1995 he survived an assassination attempt in which his attacker was taken into custody by his bodyguards. In 2006, Mengistu was sentenced to death in absentia by Ethiopia's High Court. He was found guilty of false imprisonment, homicide, and illegal confiscation of property. During his reign, the sight of students, government detractors, or rebel sympathizers hanging from lampposts was a routine spectacle. Mengistu is alleged to have personally extinguished opponents by gunning them down or garroting them, declaring that he was leading by example. It remains unclear whether Zimbabwe will permit his extradition.

MAXIMILIAN I (1832-1867) MEXICO

An Austrian interloper appointed by Napoleon III of France, Maximilian's ill-fated three-year reign was doomed from the start. Misunderstood by his Mexican subjects and mystified by the country and culture he presumed to govern, this transplanted archduke and would-be emperor was caught between the anti-imperialist native forces of Benito Juarez and his own arrogance and presumption. After his capture and execution by a Juarista firing squad, his wife, the Empress Carlotta, went insane and never recovered.

Maximilian I

MICHEL MICOMBERO (1940-1983) BURUNDI

Both Burundi and Rwanda are traditional sites for warfare between the Tutsi and Hutu tribes, who regularly engage in massacres and counter-massacres, feuding on a shocking scale. One particularly appalling Burundi massacre of Tutsis was described by President Micombero (a Tutsi) as "indescribable atrocities. Mothers with babes in arms were massacred. Mothers-to-be were treated so indescribably as to revolt human conscience." Before launching retaliatory genocide, youths went into the streets crazed with drugs, drink, and magic which they thought made them invulnerable, and vice versa in Rwanda. Michel Micombero was the first President of Burundi. He was of Tutsi ethnicity. After independence, Burundi descended into anarchy. In 1965, the Hutus launched a coup and removed the king. The predominantly Hutu police force began to systematically slaughter Tutsis. Michel Micombero was a young Tutsi army captain who had only recently returned from school in Belgium and had quickly risen to the post of Secretary of Defense. He rallied the army and its Tutsi officers against the members of the coup and gave them the boot. He then set about unleashing waves of attacks on Hutus throughout the nation. Micombero became Prime Minister in 1966 and was the power behind the throne in a nation technically ruled by King Ntare V, who deposed his father with Micombero's help. Soon thereafter, Micombero junked the monarchy and made himself president. He imposed a staunch regime of law and order, and sharply curtailed outbursts of Hutu militarism. In 1972, Hutu refugees exploded in an uprising. This was repulsed by retaliatory violence that killed some 150,000 Hutus. Micombero unquestionably played a leading role in these exterminations. Afterward, Micombero became increasingly corrupt and took consolation in the bottle. He was overthrown and died in Somalia in 1983.

SESE SEKO MOBUTU (1930-1997) ZAIRE

"Mobutuism" was Mobutu's political philosophy, which he described as "the thought, teachings and actions of Mobutu." Son of a cook and hotel maid, he changed his name from Joseph-Desire Mobutu to Sese Seko Kuku Ngbendu Wa Za Banga Mobutu, which means "the cock who leaves no hen unruffled" or, "the cock who jumps on anything that moves," and proposed to solve what he called the perpetual national "crisis" with "autocriticism." Wearing his leopard-skin cap and carrying an ivory walking stick, he was referred to in all the newspapers and official speeches as "The President Founder" and "The Guide," and frequently could be seen driving past hundreds of billboards bearing his photograph and the words, "Thank you, citizen President." Mobutu's regime was called a "kleptocracy." He had a dozen homes in Zaire, including "Versailles in the Jungle," an enormous palace ringed by dozens of satellite houses for his guards, aides, and their families, not to mention his vineyard in Portugal, 32-room mansion in Switzerland, and sixteenth-century castle in Spain. His personal fortune was estimated at $5 billion while the average Zairean citizen dwelled in a hut and earned $180 per year. Mobutu advised children to beat their parents if they criticized his government.

Sese Seko Mobutu

ROBERT MUGABE (1927-) ZIMBABWE

Robert Gabriel Mugabe is President of Zimbabwe. He served as prime minister from 1980 to 1987 and, since that time, has acted as executive head of state. During his tenure he has managed to destroy the economic health of the nation while, because of his record of "appalling mismanagement, corruption, and brutal repression," he has made himself an outcast in the community of nations. One commentator has observed that "Mugabe has ruled Zimbabwe for nearly three decades and has led it, in that time, from impressive success to the most dramatic peacetime collapse of any country since Weimar Germany." Mugabe's administration has increasingly provoked universal condemnation and his position towards Zimbabwe's white minority has been denounced as racist. Mugabe's critics accuse him of conducting a "reign of terror" whose "transgressions are unpardonable." The London *Times* has charged that Mugabe's militia murdered the wife of his chief rival by burning her alive with gasoline after chopping off her extremities. Muagabe's combat forces have decimated Ndebele tribesmen in Matabeleland and incurred displacement of occupants of shantytowns he has razed. He polices the people of Zimbabwe with his Central Intelligence Organization, breeding a culture of intimidation. Sanctions intended to isolate Mugabe have been imposed by the United States and the European Union. Citations, awards, and honorary degrees have been revoked and stripped away, out of "revulsion at the abuse of human rights and abject disregard for the democratic process in Zimbabwe over which President Mugabe has presided". Some observers have suggested that Mugabe began to misrule Zimbabwe after the death of his first wife, who was his closest confidante. His current wife Grace, because of her fondness for shopping sprees, has earned the nickname "Gucci Grace." When the US and the EU imposed a travel ban on the Mugabes, a British parliamentarian remarked, "Maybe the ban will stop Grace Mugabe going on her lavish shopping trips in the face of catastrophic poverty blighting the people of Zimbabwe." When Mugabe wriggled around the ban to travel to Vatican City for the funeral of Pope John Paul II, a scandal arose merely because Mugabe surprised Prince Charles, Prince of Wales, and shook his hand. Charles has described the Mugabe regime as "abhorrent." It has been suggested that, should Mugabe leave Zimbabwe, he might make his way to Malaysia, where it is believed that he has sequestered his wealth.

YOWERI MUSEVENI (1944-) UGANDA

Incumbent president of Uganda who has been accused of a catalog of atrocities beginning with: acts of terrorism including terrorizing the civilian population and inflicting collective punishments; unlawful killings; extreme violence to life, health, and physical or mental well-being of persons, in particular murder; sexual violence including rape and sexual slavery; outrages upon personal dignity, including violence to life, health, and physical or mental well being of persons, in particular cruel treatment; other inhumane acts such as use of child soldiers, defined as "conscripting or enlisting children under the age of fifteen years into armed forces or groups, or using them to participate actively in hostilities"; abductions and forced labor; enslavement; looting; pillaging; money laundering; and arms smuggling.

BENITO MUSSOLINI (1883-1945) ITALY

Benito Mussolini was an ideologue almost from childhood. His father steeped him in political lore from his earliest years, and even the names his parents had given him had been selected in homage to political heroes. By the time he was a teenager, Mussolini was a full-fledged agitator, eager to put his political ideas in practice. He gave stirring speeches and struck dramatic, swaggering poses. As the first Fascist party began to gel under his guidance, his followers were called "blackshirts," after their distinctive attire. When Mussolini and his blackshirts led a "March on Rome" demanding power, King Victor Emmanuel III offered him equal control of the nation. At the outset of Mussolini's rule, Fascism was a hot new trend embraced by Italy's fashionable set and cultural elite; there was an outpouring of Fascist-influenced avant-garde literature and Futurist art. Mussolini devoted much of his time to grandiose works and sponsoring art projects—he aspired to recapture the glories of ancient Rome. Adopting the honorific *Il Duce*—The Leader—he formed a "Pact of Steel" with Adolf Hitler and tried to create an empire beginning with the conquest of Ethiopia, where his homicidal and fanatic military forces committed heinous cruelties against the populace, using mustard gas and taking 30,000 Ethiopian lives. Toward the end of the Second World War, as his fortunes began to wane, he was captured by partisans who shot him along with his mistress and, after spitting on the bodies and mangling them, they hanged them upside down from meat hooks in a public square.

Benito Mussolini

Supplicants of the Nizam of Hyderabad approached him with the invocation: "After kissing the Threshold of Your Throne, it is humbly submitted to the Great and Holy Protector of the World, Shadow of God, Mighty Holder of Destinies, Full of Light and Most Elevated Among Creatures, the Exalted, may God's Shadow never grow less, may God protect Your Kingdom and Your Sultanate, most respectfully I beg to submit..."

SLOBODAN MILOSEVIC (1941-2006) SERBIA

Monstrous practitioner of ethnic cleansing, tagged the "Butcher of the Balkans." In an ugly attempt to forge an expanded Serbian bloc from the remnants of a post-soviet-era Yugoslavia, Milosevic unleashed homicidal warlords on a spree of murder, rape, and mayhem that brought UN and NATO forces directly into the devastating conflict and ultimately resulted in his trial and condemnation before the International Criminal Tribunal at the Hague.

MURAD IV (1612-1640) OTTOMAN EMPIRE

Ordered shore batteries to open fire on and sink a boatload of women on the Bosporus when their boat came too close to the Seraglio. On another occasion he drowned a party of women when he chanced to come across them in a meadow and took exception to the noise they were making. "Murad quickly found a simple panacea for the ills of the country," writes Barber. "He cut off the head of any man who came under the slightest suspicion." He executed the Grand Mufti because he was dissatisfied with the state of the roads. He beheaded his chief musician for playing a Persian air.

111

Murad liked to take his chief executioner Kara Ali into the streets looking for people whose clothes offended him; violators were summarily blinded or executed. He liked to patrol the taverns at night and if he caught anyone smoking he declared himself and dispatched the offender on the spot. When he caught one of his gardeners and his wife smoking, he had their legs amputated, and exhibited them in public in a cart while they bled to death. A Venetian who added a room to the top of his house was hanged because Murad thought he had done it to spy on the Sultan's harem. A Frenchman who arranged a date with a Turkish girl was impaled. He spent hours exercising the royal prerogative of taking ten innocent lives a day (he had passed a law which entitled him to do this) as he practiced his powers with the arquebus on passersby who were too near the palace walls. When a concubine from the harem of Murad's son was seduced by an outsider, he had all two hundred eighty girls tied in weighted sacks and tossed into the Bosporus. Murad died after a drinking bout.

N

NADIR SHAH (1688-1747) PERSIA

Bandit who became a military chieftan. Driving his armies on lightning raids, he defeated the Turks and terrified the Russians into surrender. Soon he had secured rulership of Persia, becoming shah. He multiplied his military adventures, invading northern India and laying waste the glittering city of Delhi, where he obliterated tens of thousands of inhabitants. He returned to Persia bearing fabulous treasures, including the peacock throne and the Koh-i-noor diamond. By now, Nadir's maniacal cruelty had reached deranged proportions. He fought pointless wars and futile campaigns, causing egregious suffering and bloodshed. When he suspected his son of treason, he ordered his eyes to be put out. Nadir's excesses were such that even his own soldiers regarded him with opprobrium. Nadir Shah was so enamored of violent strife that he was aghast at the concept that paradise was a place of serenity and peace. "How then," he asked, "can it be any fun?"

NAPOLEON BONAPARTE (1769-1821) FRANCE

Monomaniacal French general who crowned himself "emperor" and caused the deaths of 1,000,000 Europeans while waging wars of conquest in the name of "liberation." Though a bloody, remorseless murderer, Bonaparte is venerated as a martial hero to this day by the Republic of France, where his body lies in decorous state in the monumental atrium of the Hotel des Invalides Military Museum in Paris, entombed in three layers of insulation from the realm of the living: a bronze casing within a silver casket within a marble sarcophagus, surrounded by a vigilant ring of elegant, sculpted torches symbolizing eternal glory.

Napoleon Bonaparte

NEBUCHADNEZZAR (634 BC-500 BC) BABYLON

Conquered Judah, captured the inhabitants, and transported them
wholesale to his capital, occasioning the Babylonian Captivity. Built the
Hanging Gardens of Babylon and other architectural wonders. Went
temporarily insane and lived in the wilderness like an animal for seven
years, eating grass.

Nebuchadnezzar

NERO (37-68) ROME

Emperor of Rome. A foppish, bloated poet, he was noted, in an age of indulgence, for his extravagance and debauchery. When Rome burned, Nero hastened to put on Greek robes, then played his lyre and sang, enacting Homer's version of the fall and destruction of Troy. Scapegoating the newly-formed Christian sect for the fire, Nero had the Christians immersed in boiling pitch and turned into human torches, had them torn to pieces by dogs, or mangled by crucifixion. Nero attempted to assassinate his mother first by poison, then by having a roof collapse over her, then by providing her with a disintegrating boat, and finally succeeded by sending in swordsmen to finish her off. He murdered his wife by kicking her in the stomach when she was pregnant. He spent his days engaged with cultural pursuits, luxuriating in the company of his decadent friends and the poisoner and satirical poet Petronius, a languid authority on elegance whom Nero appointed "Arbiter of the Imperial Pleasures." Nero took a hermaphrodite "bride" named Sporus in a mock marriage ceremony followed by a wedding night in which they imitated the cries of a virgin being deflowered. He built his Golden House in the ruins of Rome destroyed by the great fire. He once ordered two senators sacrificed to avert the collision of a comet with earth. When he was forced to commit suicide, he exclaimed, "What an artist dies in me!"

Nero

The secret police force of Shah Reza Pahlavi of Iran was the dreaded SAVAK; the Iraqi secret police under Hussein was the Mukhabarat, the Baath intelligence network, guilty of obscene atrocities, torture, and execution; Hussein maintained two additional police forces: the Amn, or civilian state security bureau, and the Estikhbarat, the military intelligence wing; OBAN was the acronym of the Brazilian death squad; Ochrana was the name of the Russian secret police (under Tzar Nicholas)—it then became the Cheka under Lenin and Stalin, who introduced the gulags, which replaced the Tzarist era Siberian penal colonies, followed by the OGPU, which was renamed NKVD and finally, KGB; "National Information Services" was the Orwellian name of Brazil's secret police; and ORDEN was the Salvadoran anti-communist terror squad.

FRANCISCO MACIAS NGUEMA (1924-1979) EQUATORIAL GUINEA

First President of Equatorial Guinea, from 1968 until his overthrow in 1979. Born the son of a witch doctor who reportedly killed his younger brother, he failed the civil service exam three times, then ran for president and defeated Prime Minister Bonifacio Ondó Edu who went briefly into exile in Gabon and was executed soon after his return on trumped-up charges of planning a coup. His country has been referred to as "a vast concentration camp" infected by malaria, fiariasis, infectious hepatitis, dysentery and whooping cough, tuberculosis, and parasitic intestinal diseases. The savagery of Francisco Macías Nguema Biyogo Negue Ndong, "President for Life, Major General of the Armed Forces, and Great Maestro of Popular Education, Science and Traditional Culture" strains the imagination. In 1971, Macías Nguema issued Decree 415, which repealed parts of the 1968 Constitution and granted him "all direct powers of Government and Institutions," including powers formerly held by the legislative and judiciary branches, as well as the cabinet of ministers. Later the same year, Law 1 imposed the death penalty as punishment for threatening the President or the government. Insulting or offending the President or his cabinet was punishable by 30 years in prison. In 1972, a presidential decree merged all existing political parties into the United National Party with Macías Nguema as President for Life. Macías Nguema declared private education subversive, and banned it entirely with Decree 6; By Macías' official decree slavery was reintroduced to his country in 1976. The president's paranoid actions included banning use of the word "intellectual" and destroying boats to stop his people fleeing from his rule (fishing was banned). The only road out of the country on the mainland was also mined. He banned Western medicines, stating that they were "un-African." He "Africanized" his name to Masie Nguema Biyogo Ñegue Ndong in 1976 after demanding that the rest of the Equatoguinean population do the same. During his presidency, his country was nicknamed "the Dachau of Africa." More than a third of Equatorial Guinea's population fled to other countries to escape his brutal reign. He was known to order entire families and villages executed. Macías Nguema made himself the focus of an extreme personality cult, perhaps fueled by his consumption of copious amounts of bhang and iboga (hallucinogenic drugs), and assigned himself titles such as the "Unique Miracle" and "Grand Master of Education, Science, and Culture." During Macías Nguema's regime, the country had neither a development plan nor an accounting system for government funds. After killing the governor of the Central Bank, he carried everything that remained in the national treasury to his house in a rural village. During Christmas of 1975 he ordered about 150 of his opponents killed. Soldiers executed them in the Malabo football stadium while amplifiers were playing *Those Were the Days*. By 1979, Macías Nguema's brutality had led to condemnations from the United Nations and European Commission. That summer, Macías Nguema executed several members of his own family, leading members of his inner circle to fear that he had become altogether irrational. In 1979 he was overthrown by his nephew Teodoro Obiang Nguema Mbasogo. The deposed ruler and a contingent of loyal forces initially resisted the coup, but his forces eventually abandoned him, and he was captured in a forest. A military tribunal convened to try Macías Nguema and several members of his regime. The charges for the ten defendants included genocide, mass murder, embezzlement of public funds, violations of human rights, and treason. Nguema was sentenced to death "101 times" and executed by a Moroccan firing squad at Black Beach Prison. Macías Nguema was responsible for the deaths of anywhere from 50,000 to 80,000 people. One observer has noted that this was proportionally worse than the Nazis' rampage through Europe. He has been compared to Pol Pot because of the violent, unpredictable, and anti-intellectual nature of both regimes: government fit only to be described as kakistocracy.

TEODORO OBIANG NGUEMA (1942-) EQUITORIAL GUINEA

Macías Nguema's nephew and successor Teodoro Obiang Nguema Mbasogo has governed Equitorial Guinea for the past thirty-three years. Abuses under Obiang have included "unlawful killings by security forces; government-sanctioned kidnappings; systematic torture of prisoners and detainees by security forces; life-threatening conditions in prisons and detention facilities; impunity; arbitrary arrest, detention, and incommunicado detention." His opponents have accused him of cannibalism—specifically, of eating parts of his opponents to gain "power." In 2003, state-operated radio declared Obiang "the country's god" who had "all power over men and things." It added that the president was "in permanent contact with the Almighty" and "can decide to kill with-

Saparmurat Niyazov

Niyazov that rotated in such a way as to be always facing the sun. He shut down libraries with the explanation that the only books worth reading were the Koran and his autobiography. He closed all hospitals lying outside the capital, Asgabat, so that patients would come to the city for medical attention, and he required physicians to swear an oath to him that would replace the Oath of Hippocrates. He rewrote the national anthem, adding passages referring to himself. He revoked pensions for the elderly and demanded that those who had received pensions should refund them. He banished dogs from city streets because of their "unappealing odor." He built an ice skating rink in the capital so desert dwellers could learn to skate. He dismissed the entire work force of the national health system on a whim, and outlawed tobacco, opera, ballet, long hair, beards, makeup, lip-synching, and gold teeth. He advised persons with dental problems to take a lesson from dogs, and strengthen their teeth by gnawing on bones.

KWAME NKRUMAH (1909-1972) GHANA

Prototypical African autocrat whose alarmingly repressive regime saw several assassination attempts and ultimately incurred his overthrow. Nkrumah was an admired model for several African dictators who followed.

MANUEL NORIEGA (1934-) PANAMA

Manuel Noriega of Panama was a practitioner of Candomble, Voodoo, Santeria, and Palo Mayombe, and regularly sought the counsel of witches. The prediction by Noriega's favorite witch-advisor that the US invasion would take place one day later than it did resulted in his capture. When US commandos raided his headquarters, they found evidence that he had been casting spells, as well as a freezer containing totems put inside as a means of "freezing" the actions of his enemies. Among his other personal items were "altars of power," through which black magic worshippers believe spirits can manipulate mortal fate.

Manuel Noriega

O

OMAR BONGO ONDIMBA (1935-2009) GABON

Omar Bongo was one of the wealthiest men in the world, his affluence being chiefly attributable to ill-gotten petrochemical income. The five foot tall Gabonese president, who often wore platform shoes, wasn't lacking in stature: As the namesake of Gabon's Bongo Airport, Bongo Hospital, Bongo University, Bongo Stadium, and Bongo Auditorium, he needed no artificial aggrandizement. His primary residence was the $800 million presidential palace in Libreville while his supplemental real estate holdings included dozens of penthouses, villas, and other elegant properties scattered around Paris and the rest of his beloved France. He maintained a limousine fleet and owned a stable of expensive and exotic vehicles ranging from a Maybach bought for his wife to a Ferrari GT bought for his son and a Ferrari Scaglietti kept for his personal use. A US Senate report issued in the late 1990s stated that his family spent $100 million annually. All this conspicuous prosperity had its origins in an oil boom that amply financed the entire Gabonese economy. The residue from the flood of petrodollars sustained a bloated bureaucracy and a formerly impoverished populace in a style usually associated with a Persian Gulf emirate. With 2,500,000,000 barrels of oil reserves on tap, Bongo could afford to live large and he did just that, shrewdly steering the Gabonese ship of state for more than forty fruitful years. He funded grandiose projects like the Trans-Gabon Railway, which penetrated the green fastnesses of the unspoiled interior. In 2002, in a much-publicized incident, the sixty-seven-year-old president flubbed an attempt at seducing a twenty-two-year-old Peruvian beauty queen he had invited to Gabon to officiate at a pageant. She was horrified when she found that, upon arrival at the presidential palace, Bongo led her into a luxurious, hidden bedroom revealed at the push of a button by the retraction of a pair of sliding doors. Aghast, she vehemently protested the implications of the situation and fled to a downtown hotel. Had she known the president better, she wouldn't have been surprised. Bongo had sired, with his wife and others, more than thirty children, at home and abroad...

OTHO (32 - 69) ROME

Marcus Salvius Otho, whose wife Poppaea was coveted by his friend the Emperor Nero; she proclaimed that she would allow herself to be possessed by him only on the condition that she should be made empress. Nero married her and she died three years later when Nero kicked her in the stomach while she was pregnant.

> Maria Peron, second wife of perennial dictator Juan Peron, governed Argentina through the advice of her astrologer, the occultist Jose Lopez Rega, and ended up in a naval hospital hoarding barbiturates for periodic suicide attempts.

P

MOHAMMAD REZA PAHLAVI (1919-1980) IRAN

SAVAK (Samane Etelaat va Amniate Kechvar, or Security and Intelligence Organization) was the notorious secret police apparatus of the Shah Pahlavi. The influence of SAVAK was felt and feared throughout Iran and as far away as the US, where it was headed by spymaster Mozafar Rafizadeh, who persecuted anti-Shah Iranians, gathered intelligence, and reputedly organized orgies and opium parties at the Iranian Embassy in Washington to subvert American senators and congressmen. The Shah implemented drug control measures by instructing his Bureau of Public Health to offer addicts unlimited free supplies of a potent, pleasure-inducing narcotic (Drug X) containing substances (which came to be known on the street as "ingredients of persuasion") that effectively killed the user within a short time.

Mohammad Reza Pahlavi

Benito Mussolini outlawed publication of photos or drawings of skinny women in Italian newspapers, ads, and government publications under threat of jail.

PARYSATIS (?-395 BC) PERSIA

Vindictive queen who patiently, methodically, and ruthlessly plotted the assassination of a despised satrap she held responsible for the death of her favorite son.

Parysatis

ALI PASHA (1744-1822) OTTOMAN EMPIRE

"When he traveled his harem was called his 'hen-coop on wheels,' always well-stocked with beautiful girls brutally torn from their fathers, lovers, and husbands. Ali rarely paid any attention to the niceties of courtship. When he saw a woman he wanted, his soldiers carted her off to the palace, and that was that. If her family objected, he had their house burned down and its residents killed. On the other hand, Ali loved handsome boys, and had quite a stable of these Ganymedes. His foster brother and henchman, the 'Blood Drinker,' was a monster who wore out the executioners, who complained of fatigue. He threw his victims into a leopard's cage, burned them alive, or had their bones broken by soldiers jumping on a board laid on top of them, and finally cemented into containers with only their heads protruding."

PEDRO THE CRUEL (1334-1369) SPAIN

Spanish king who managed to anger, irritate, annoy, and antagonize everyone with whom he came in contact, and who made implacable enemies of England, France, the Vatican, and the nobility of his own country. He murdered three of his four brothers—the fourth surviving to murder Pedro in turn.

JUAN PERON (1893-1974) ARGENTINA

The notoriety of Argentinian dictator Juan Peron has been curiously eclipsed by the legend of his extraordinary wife, Eva Duarte, popularly known as Evita. Upon her death, the body of Argentina's beloved peon-to-princess first lady, whose life has been celebrated in a hit musical, was expertly embalmed and preserved with all its organs and internals, and the attending embalmer made wax and vinyl casts of her cadaver. The body was initially displayed in public in Buenos Aires while husband Juan prepared a magnificent monument to house the remains. But when he was overthrown by a military coup, his successors wanted to rid the country of all things Peron, and they ensconced the body in an attic, then arranged to have it secretly buried in Italy. Following another coup twenty years later, the new Argentine government, in exchange for Juan Peron's political endorsement, exhumed the remains and shipped them to him in Madrid, where he then was living. "He reportedly kept the body first in an open casket on the dining room table, and then in a shrine in his cellar. There are creepy stories of his third wife, Isabel, combing the corpse's hair and lying on top of, or in, the coffin. The body was finally brought back to Argentina in 1974, when Isabel Peron assumed control of the country on the death of her husband, who had returned to Argentina the year before to serve a third term as president. Eva Peron's remains are now buried in a Buenos Aires tomb, located beneath two trap doors. Eva's tomb has become a shrine and a place of pilgrimage. As for Juan Peron, vandals broke into his tomb in 1987 and sawed off his hands in a mysterious incident that has yet to be explained."

Juan Peron

PHALARIS (570 BC-554 BC) SICILY

Cruel Agrigentian tyrant who burned his victims alive in a brazen bull (making his first experiment upon Perillus, its inventor)—the cries representing the bellowing of the bull.

JOSEF PILSUDSKI (1867-1935) POLAND

Charismatic but controversial Josef Piludski was a Polish field marshal who headed the national government during the 1920s and 1930s. He staged a coup d'etat, adopted supralegal measures, harassed opponents, and built special penitentiaries to house political prisoners. In one of the most reviled of these penitentiaries, Bereza Kartuska Detention Camp, prisoners were grossly mistreated. He sent armed troops into the Sejm—the Polish parliament—when he suspected a vote would not go his way. His death was occasioned by a lavish funeral and his body toured Poland on a funeral train, after which it was publicly displayed for two years at the Crypt of the Silver Bells in a Warsaw cathedral. Streets, ships, racehorses, and even an armored train were christened after him and coins and postage stamps also perpetuate his name. His brain was donated to a university for scientific study, and his heart was buried in his mother's grave.

Josef Pilsudski

Recently in Uruguay (described as a military Frankenstein and a political morgue) you could be arrested for your smile or sent to jail for ten years on account of "political inclinations." If you wanted to read a back issue of a newspaper, you had to go to the police, declare your intentions, identify the article, and prove its ideological compatibility with the regime. Inquiring journalists were immediately locked up as spies. Uruguay's OCOA (anti-subversive operations coordinating organization) and SID (defense intelligence service) assassination squads brazenly eliminated opponents in foreign countries.

AUGUSTO PINOCHET (1915-2006) CHILE

Died at the age of ninety-one, escaping justice for abuses of his seventeen year regime. Weeping supporters gathered in front of the Santiago Military Hospital where he died, chanting "long live Pinochet" while passing motorists shouted insults at them. After he retired, his millions of dollars in secret offshore bank accounts were exposed. He owed ten million dollars in unpaid taxes and was indicted for tax evasion. The Chilean Supreme Court took him to task, holding him responsible for the disappearance of five hundred dissidents arrested by the secret police. Most had been killed, and their bodies flung into the sea. More than three thousand political murders blacken the record of Pinochet's term. The mustachioed general propelled himself to national leadership with the 1973 coup that ousted his predecessor Salvador Allende who, as his presidential palace came under aerial bombardment, committed suicide using a submachine gun given him by Fidel Castro. Pinochet unfurled a drag-net to snare Allende sympathizers and quash residual leftist elements. He sent tanks and armored personnel carriers rumbling through Santiago's streets, arresting likely suspects and ushering them into a soccer stadium, hurriedly converted into a detention center, where many were tortured and executed. Sweeps by death squads netted other "enemies" who were trucked to the Atacama Desert in a "Caravan of Death" to be summarily shot and dumped in unmarked graves. In addition to the dead, more than 1,000 victims remain unaccounted for. Pinochet disbanded Congress, banned political activity, and crushed dissent. "Not a leaf moves in this country if I'm not moving it," he said. Pinochet defended his draconian exploits as a crusade to free society from communism. Claiming partial credit for the collapse of the Soviet bloc, he declared, "I see myself as a good angel." At the height of his regime, when investigators discovered coffins into each of which two bodies had been crammed, Pinochet dismissed the matter, saying it seemed "a good cemetery space-saving measure." When Pinochet died in 2006, his family considered conventional burial too risky, since the family grave reserved for him in Santiago would invite vandalism. Consequently, his remains were cremated and his ashes scattered at his country estate at Los Boldos. At last glance, the abandoned estate had become a marijuana plantation.

POL POT (1925-1998) CAMBODIA

A Buddhist monk and electronics student who became an insane monster, imposing on a helpless nation a system of communist atavism based on the demented theories of fellow student Khieu Samphan that Cambodia must regress to a peasant economy (rural), without towns, without industry, without currency, and without education. The capital, Phnom Penh, was evacuated—virtually emptied—as three million citizens were deprived of their possessions and ordered out of their homes; irrespective of whether they were old, sick, pregnant, crippled, newly born, or dying, they were marched into the countryside and herded into vast communes to work in the fields. Many died of exhaustion or starvation. Everyone got a bowl of gruel each day, one sleeping mat, and a one pair of black overalls each year. There was no property, and no trade, and no money, which was abolished. Schools and colleges, too, were abolished. Books were burned; Kampuchea (Cambodia) became "The Land of the Walking Dead." The educated classes were liquidated by bayonet or pickaxe, as were priests, prison inmates, and defeated soldiers of the former regime. Anyone who complained or criticized the system was summarily clubbed to death. Starving peasants found cannibalizing dead bodies were buried to their necks in sand and left to die; their heads would be cut off and stuck on poles to serve as a warning to others. The extermination continued for four years with no hope of help from the outside world. Half the total population of the country died from disease, starvation, neglect, brutalization, murder, or massacre.

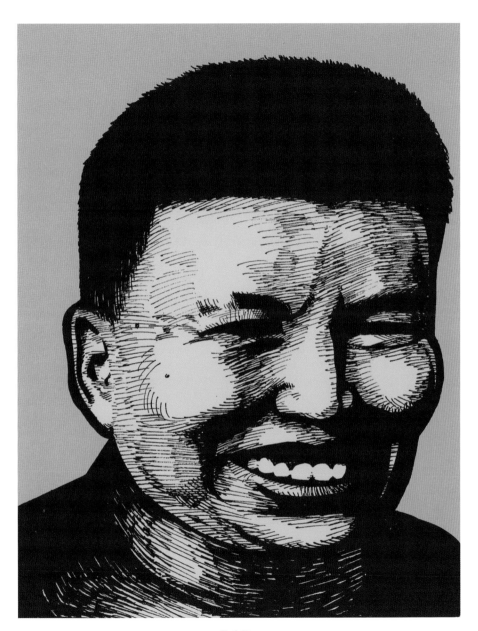

Pol Pot

CHUNG-HEE PARK (1917-1979) SOUTH KOREA

Had evangelist Reverend Moon do fund-raising campaigns for him. He directed "Operation White Snow" to spread around hundreds of thousands of dollars in bribes to US politicians in the 1970s. He enacted Emergency Measure No. 9, declared martial law, secured his position as President for Life, and instituted the Yushin constitution, forbidding all opposition. By the late 1970s, Park's widespread unpopularity was clear. Violent demonstrations erupted throughout the country and contributed to a sense of urgency. An assassination tango began in which a commando unit fielded by North Korea reached the doorstep of Park's presidential residence, the Blue House, before being neutralized in a ferocious gun battle with South Korean police. In response, the South Korean government organized its own field unit with the aim of assassinating North Korean leader Kim Il-sung. In 1974, as Park was giving a speech in the National Theater in Seoul, a North Korean agent fired at Park from the front row, missing the president but killing his wife and a singer. Finally, in 1979, the director of Park's own Korean Central Intelligence Agency shot and killed him along with several bodyguards. The killer stated that his only motive had been patriotism.

> Under the rule of the monster Ceaucescu, the Romanian populace referred to their capital, Bucharest, as "Paranopolis."

POLYCRATES (?-522 BC) SAMOS

Maritime tyrant who plundered the Greek coast and the Mediterranean with a fleet of forty triremes fitted with battering rams. Flagrantly hedonistic, he populated his court with poets and singers, and built a luxurious pleasure district in his capital, designed to rival the park at Sardis called "Sweet Embrace." Offering innumerable temptations and blandishments, its lanes were lined with professional women and with shops and stalls presenting the finest culinary delights available and entirely given over to sensuality and incontinence of every kind. When the Egyptian king remarked that the gods envied Polycrates, the latter appealed to a soothsayer, who advised him to discard some precious object held dear. Polycrates removed his ring and cast it into the sea. When, a few days later, he discovered the ring in the belly of a fish he had been served, he construed ill omen and, sure enough, was soon thereafter trapped and done in by his adversaries. In psychiatry, the term "Polycrates complex" refers to a condition in which guilt prompts a subconscious desire to be caught and punished.

Iran's Ayatollah Khomeini decreed the specifics of correct bathroom hygiene, including the acceptable method for holding toilet paper and which hand to use when performing personal ablutions.

Debauched Roman Caesar Caligula invited noblemen to his imperial banquets, then forced himself on their wives and afterward publicly critiqued the sexual performance of each. He served wildly extravagant meals consisting of such oddities as bread loaves made of gold and wine spiked with dissolved pearls. He whimsically built artificial mountains on level plains and lopped off the peaks of real mountains so that he could construct fantasy palaces concocted in his dreams. He capriciously condemned men to confinement in cramped cages or ordered them sawn in two if they failed to swear by his genius.

Q

MUAMMAR QADDAFI (1942-2011) LIBYA

Defiant, eccentric, and mercurial, this reckless, renegade, self-styled "Brother Leader" ruled Libya for forty-two years, executing by public hanging anyone brazen enough to oppose him. A loose cannon, he twice shot down civilian airliners, funded international terrorism, and bombed a discoteque frequented by American servicemen. Because Libyans were going outside the country for medical treatment, he commanded Tripoli's foremost medical school to accept 2,000 new applicants, regardless of qualifications. He renamed the months, as in the case of January which, on account of its coldness, he renamed Where is the Fire? He was especially noted for his extravagant wardrobe which included elaborate military uniforms, Bedouin robes, garish Hawaiian shirts, flashy leisure suits, onyx-black aviator sunglasses, and lapel pins in the shape of the African continent. When he traveled abroad, he would pitch an enomorous Arab tent outdoors on the grounds of whatever foreign capital he happened to be visiting. The tent, which he claimed was bulletproof, weighed so much and was so cumbersome that it had to be transported by a separate plane. To complete the picture, Qaddafi would occasionally bring along a camel or two. He was afraid of elevators and would climb stairs only to a height of thirty-five steps. He had an all-female virgin bodyguard. This colorful retinue took a vow of chastity upon entering Qaddafi's service. Handpicked by Brother Leader, these modern-day Amazons trained at an all-female military academy, wore ornate uniforms, sassy makeup, and distinctive high-heeled combat boots. He had a voluptuous Ukrainian nurse who attended him for a decade and who also served him as a personal aide. She, along with several other nurses, referred to him as "Daddy." A seventeen-year-old Italian prostitute told the press that she had learned from attending an orgy held by Qaddafi a mysterious ritual practice of his harem he called "bunga bunga." He was infatuated with US Secretary of State Condoleezza Rice, to whom he referred as "my black African darling." In his fortified Tripoli stronghold, with its maze of escape tunnels, he maintained, like a schoolboy with a crush, a shrine adorned with photographs and keepsakes pertaining to Rice. He lavished expensive gifts on her when she visited him there. He put in wide circulation the fruit of his wit and wisdom in the form of his *Green Book*, an ideological manifesto which outlined his "Third International Theory" of government and social order. After rebels defeated his military forces and drove him from his last defensive bastion, he was trapped like a rat in a sewer. Dragged by rebel forces from his hiding place in the mouth of a filthy, rubbish-strewn drainage pipe, the stinking, bedraggled Brother Leader was hastened to a nearby pickup truck with his hairpiece dislodged, and he was shot like a rabid dog as his captors rejoiced, shouting "Allahu Akbar!"—God is great! Within days Libyan schoolchildren were publicly chanting slogans against their kooky former leader and hanging him in effigy. Thrilled at being able to dispense with Qaddafi's crackpot notions of Jamahiriya—a utopia ruled by the masses—they no longer had to start the day with a pledge of allegiance to the "Frizzhead"—an insult referring to Qaddafi's weirdo shocklocks, or with lessons that included instruction from the *Green Book* and study of the "mind of Qaddafi."

Saddam Hussein, the "Butcher of Baghdad," inspired hot-selling toilet tissue with his face printed on it, and prompted Italian politician and porn princess Cicciolina to publicly offer to have sex with him in exchange for release of hostages.

Muammar Qaddafi

Rome's Heliogabalus was the high priest presiding over a cult of phallic worship. One of the cult's rituals involved toasting the severed genitals of sacrificial victims over the flames of a sacred fire. He was a cross-dressing corybant who solemnly pranced around an altar to the sound of flutes and tambourines, and he begged his physicians to "make him into a woman, promising them large sums should they succeed."

Romanian Vlad Tepes rounded up indigents and incinerated them in a barn so that there would be "no poor people" in his country.

In a rage over the death of one of his wives during a botched abortion, Ugandan strongman Idi Amin ordered surgeons to decapitate and dismember the woman, then reattach her head backwards on her torso, while fastening her legs to her shoulder sockets and her arms to her hips. He then displayed the mutilated corpse to his surviving wife as a grisly warning against misbehavior.

R

RAMSES II (1292 BC-1225 BC) EGYPT

Vainglorious pharoah of the Bible who usurped power from his brother, waged expansionist wars, and built splendid edifices, including some of the great pyramids, the magnificent temples at Luxor and Karnak, the Ramseum, his magnificent mortuary at Thebes, and similar colossi, all built by miserably enslaved peoples.

Ramses II

Ghana maximum leader Acheampong was officially known as "Head of State, Head of the Supreme Military Council, Chairman of the National Redemption Council and Minister of Defense, Finance and Cocoa Affairs."

JUAN MANUEL DE ROSAS (1793-1877) ARGENTINA

A ruthless tyrant who concocted the "Sum of Public Power"—a principle by which the powers of the legislature, the civil service, and the military are combined and delegated to the executive office. The Sum of Public Power endowed Rosas with immunity from being deposed, from criticism or dissent, and from punishment. It granted him the authority to rule the life or death of people, to enact law governing people and property, to declare war or peace with other countries, to set taxes, to designate ministers, and so forth. Rosas put the Sum of Public Power in practice assisted by spies, sycophantic propagandists, and the Mazorca (a secret political society that degenerated into a band of assassins) and, in the process, created a climate of terror. He was was adulated and fawned on in public but behind this cosmetic façade lurked a society in turmoil. Plots were hatched against him and General Justo Jose de Urquiza mounted an army with the purpose of dethroning Rosas and enacting a constitution. Roundly defeated by Urquiza, Rosas lived out his days in exile in England, as a farmer in Southampton.

NICHOLAS ROMANOV II (1868-1918) RUSSIA

Last Tzar of Russia, scion of a family that had ruled the nation for three hundred years, and supreme overlord of the antiquated and inhumane feudal system of serfdom, by the terms of which landless peasants had less value than livestock at the same time that political rights were denied and economic inequities were rife throughout Russian society as a whole. In 1917, exhausted by the privations of war and appalled and contemptuous of the influence wielded over the Tzarina by the "mad monk" Grigori Rasputin, the malignant and mysterious "power behind the throne," insurrectionists rose up against Nicholas and the rest of the Romanov clan and murdered them in the throes of the Bolshevik Revolution.

Nicholas Romanov II

Fidel Castro requires every Cuban citizen to be regularly tested for AIDS, isolates AIDS patients in a prison in Santiago de Las Vegas, and keeps them there until they die.

CARLOS HUMBERTO ROMERO (1924-) EL SALVADOR

Came to power through massive electoral fraud, during which his gangs put "tamales in the tank" (stuffed ballot boxes) while "giving lessons" to "little birds" (roughed up voting inspectors, and added the names of 300,000 dead people to the voting lists).

Pot-bellied potentate Anastasio Somoza, "El Jefe Supremo" of Nicaragua, unquestionably guilty of sickening self-deification, was also accused of running a profitable sideline in blood-smuggling.

S

ANTONIO SALAZAR (1889-1970) PORTUGAL

Mousy, quiet, and rather dull, Antonio de Oliveira Salazar was a drab and colorless homebody who dominated Portugal for thirty-six years with his para-fascist, neo-colonialist *Estado Novo*, or "New State," rule. Salazar's teachings and values where known as *A Lição de Salazar* (Salazar's Lesson) and his regime was a rigidly authoritarian one based on an orthodox interpretation of Catholic social doctrine. After an assassination attempt in which his Buick was bombed, he used an armored Chrysler Imperial as a state car. Salazar relied heavily on his secret police, first the PVDE (State Defence and Surveillance Police) and later the PIDE (International Police for State Defense). The Estado Novo's police were called DGS (General Security Directorate). The job of the secret police, of course, was to regulate political opposition and internal threats to the state. "A number of prisons were set up by Salazar's right-wing authoritarian regime where opponents of Estado Novo were sent. The Tarrafal in Cape Verde archipelago was one of them. Anarchists, communists, African separatists and guerrillas, and other opponents of Salazar's regime died or were held captive for many years in such institutions." For the final two years of his life, after he had suffered a serious stroke and been relieved of office while in a coma, those attending him humored him in the idea that he was still controlling the fate of the nation.

ANTONIO LOPEZ DE SANTA ANNA (1794-1876) MEXICO

Santa Anna was the proverbial bad penny. Repeatedly defeated both in war and in peace, he kept forever "coming back." An opportunistic

155

soldier, Santa Anna first seized dictatorial control of Mexico in 1834, and thereafter held presidency of Mexico eleven separate times in twenty-two years. In 1853, he declared himself "Dictator for Life" but a year later was removed from office for the last time. As the extent of his corruption was exposed, he was tried in absentia for treason—all his estates were confiscated by the government. He was something of an ogre in the eyes of Texans because of his harsh treatment of freedom fighters at the battles of the Alamo and Goliad. Dandified and vain, he basked in the epithets "The Eagle" and "His Serene Highness," which were attached to him. His hobbies were cockfighting and collecting Napoleonic artifacts. He was indirectly responsible for the development of chewing gum, invented by American entrepreneur Thomas Adams while experimenting with a ton of chicle he had bought from Santa Anna with hopes of finding a substitute for rubber.

Antonio Lopez de Santa Anna

SARGON (2340 BC-2305 BC) AKKAD

One of the earliest empire builders in recorded history. Sargon was a mighty conqueror who projected his dominion in the Mesopotamian region over an unprecedented extent. He ferried booty on barges, led captive monarchs in dog collars, commanded his soldiers to cleanse their swords in the sea to prove the geographical reach of his empire, and, according to ancient records, marched on cities and left them in a heap of ruins "so that there was not left even so much as a perch for a bird."

IBN SAUD (1880-1953) SAUDI ARABIA

Desert raider who created the kingdom of Saudi Arabia after he and his small band of followers scaled the battlements of Riyadh using palm trees and captured first that city, then the holy city of Mecca. Saud founded a kingdom which, to the present day, is operated like a medieval caliphate. Although slavery was officially abolished in Saudi Arabia in 1962, at which time there were 30,000 slaves in the country, including 4,000 owned by the government, it is widely rumored to still be practiced. Alcohol consumption is banned throughout Saudi Arabia, as are political parties and trade unions; strikers have been beaten to death; women are forbidden to drive; the Mutawain, or religious police, have been known to ransack homes, smashing phonographs and movie projectors with batons, and physically chastising those found smoking in public or exposing too much flesh; Christmas trees and beauty parlors are proscripted; the sexes are segregated on buses by steel partitions; and photographs are censored at processing labs. Public flogging is standard punishment for offenses ranging from traffic violations to whistling at girls. Court-ordered amputation or disfigurement is prescribed for more serious crimes. In Saudi Arabia, citizens are required by law to be Moslem. Freedoms of religion, speech, and assembly do not exist.

HAILE SELASSIE (1892-1975) ETHIOPIA

Born Tafari Makonnen. When he became emperor, he assumed the moniker Haile Selassie, meaning power of the trinity, and claimed to be the 111th descendent of King Solomon and the Queen of Sheba to rule Ethiopia. His Imperial Majesty the Conquering Lion of the Tribe of Judah, Haile Selassie I, Elect of God, Emperor of Ethiopia ruled his ancient Abyssinian realm as an anachronistic autocrat. In an archaic, backward, rural, and illiterate country where, at the dawn of the twentieth century, more than 2,000 languages and dialects were spoken, five-foot- four-inch Selassie embodied a splendid sense of theatricality, arraying himself in extravagant costumes and capes, guarded around the clock by lions and cheetahs, and accompanied at all times by an entourage of fawning chamberlains and unctuous flunkies. "He took seriously the doctrine of the divine right of kings, and he never allowed his subjects to forget that he considered himself the Elect of God." And at his ouster he was popularly accused as an exploiter who had secretly sent billions of dollars to private bank accounts abroad. As he tooled around the capital, Addis Ababa, in his fleet of Rolls Royces, the crowds who once prostrated themselves in the dust as he passed now jeered, "Thief! Thief!"

Haile Selassie

SELIM THE GRIM (1465-1520) OTTOMAN EMPIRE

Ottoman Sultan. A strangler who systematically executed most of his male relatives by having them garroted with a bow string. He convened courts in which justice was swift: Trials took just long enough for Selim to proclaim, "Kill him!"

SENNACHERIB (705 BC-681 BC) ASSYRIA

Conqueror of much of the known world of his time. Sennacherib sudued Babylon and erected the great city of Ninevah, largely built by a labor force consisting of slaves captured during his military expeditions. His planned invasion of Egypt was foiled when an immense infestation of mice nibbled away his archers' bowstrings and the quivers for their arrows.

MOHAMED SIAD BARRE (1919-1995) SOMALIA

Mohamed Siad Barre was the military dictator and President of the Somali Democratic Republic from 1969 to 1991. During his rule, he titled himself "Comrade Siad." The Barre-led military junta that seized power after a *coup d'état* in 1969 called itself the Supreme Revolutionary Council and pledged it would adopt scientific socialism as a creed for Somalia based on the model of China. Volunteer labor planted and harvested crops, and developed highways and hospitals. Businesses, banks, and industry were nationalized, and cooperative farming was encouraged. A new language was also instituted. To disseminate it along with the message of the revolution, schools were shut down and students were dispatched to rural areas to illuminate their nomadic countrymen. Barre incarcerated members of the former government, banned political parties, dissolved the parliament and the Supreme Court, and suspended the constitution. The government introduced National Security Law No. 54, which accorded the National Security Service the power to arrest and detain indefinitely anyone expressing critical opinions of the government, without ever being brought to trial. It further gave the NSS the power to arrest without a warrant anyone suspected of a crime involving "national security" and capital punishment was mandatory for anyone convicted of such acts. "Summary killings, arbitrary arrest, detention in squalid conditions, torture, rape, crippling constraints on freedom of movement and expression and a pattern of psychological intimidation" were reported by Amnesty International, which went on to report that "torture methods committed by Barre's National Security Service (NSS) included executions and beatings while tied in a contorted position, electric shocks, rape of female prisoners, simulated executions and death threats." Barre's elite unit, the Red Berets, and the paramilitary unit called the Victory Pioneers carried out systematic terror against several Somali clans. The Red Berets destroyed reservoirs supplying water to nomadic clans and their herds. More than 7,000 died of thirst. The Victory Pioneers raped large numbers of women, and more than 300,000 nomads fled to Ethiopia. Although Barre suffered life-threatening injuries in an automobile collision near Mogadishu, he continued in office until ousted in 1991. Barre was forced into exile in Kenya, but opposition groups protested his presence and, within weeks, he moved to Nigeria. He died in Lagos in 1995. His remains were buried in his homeland. He had once prophetically proclaimed, "I came to power with a gun; only the gun can make me go."

JAI SINGH (1688-1743) INDIA

Loathed all dogs and killed them on sight. He entertained himself and guests by tethering goats to a table on the lawn and watching from his palace veranda as trained leopards killed them. He used the babies of his subjects as tiger bait during his hunts (while reassuring mothers that he never missed). He collected cars, which he bought in threes, and always blue in color—when he tired of them, he had them driven out to the countryside and ceremoniously buried. Disappointed by the performance of his pony during a polo match, he publicly doused the animal with gasoline and set it ablaze. When he died, he was dressed in one of his finest suits and, wearing sunglasses, and seated in the back seat of his favorite car, a 1924 gold-plated Lanchester, he was conducted with a full funeral cortege to his final resting place.

> Iraqi government representatives asked a cryonics firm about freezing semen samples and tissue of Saddam Hussein.

ALI SOILIH (1937-1978) COMOROS

Hired a French mercenary to help him overthrow the Comorian president so he could take his place. Having succeeded in this endeavor, he immediately set about implementing reforms. He abolished the *Anda*, or Grand Wedding, along with traditional funerary rituals which were adjudged overly opulent. He lowered the voting age to fourteen and elevated teenagers to positions of authority, legalized the use of cannabis, and did away with the compulsory use of the veil by women. Soilih created the Moissy, a young revolutionary militia trained by Tanzanian military advisers. Patterned after Mao Tse-tung's Red Guards, their modus operandi was similar to that of their Chinese counterparts. Moissy units terrorized villages and specialized in violent attacks against conservative elders, formerly revered old men. The teenage Moissy were perceived as a repressive political police, and their intimidation tactics and unpredictable behavior sparked widespread resentment among the general population. Humiliation of Comorians at the hands of the Moissy deeply alienated and sharply offended the traditional leaders of the Comoros who resented the erosion of their authority and the subversion of age-old traditions. Soilih appointed a fifteen-year-old boy to run the police department, torched government records, and, when a witch doctor told him he would be killed by a white man with a black dog, destroyed every black dog on the island. Burgeoning dissatisfaction spawned repeated coup attempts against the regime. In 1978, Soilih was unseated by a European mercenary team having only fifty participants. Colonel Bob Denard, the leader of the assault, landed quietly at night and proceeded to the palace to find Soilih in bed with three girls watching a pornographic movie. He shot him, and the next morning drove through the town with Soilih's body draped over the hood of his Jeep. Denard also had with him a black German shepherd dog.

ANASTASIO SOMOZA DEBAYLE (1925-1980)

Third in a line of dynastic despots, Anastasio Somoza II perpetuated the legacy of a family that ran Nicaragua for half a century. Nicknamed "Tachito," his family owned the national airline, the national shipping company, banks, hotels, radio, television, and the press, as well as most of the manufacturing sector. Upon taking power in a corrupt electoral contest, Somoza casually remarked to his opponent, "You won the election, but I won the count." A biomedical firm called Plasmaferesis, partly owned by Somoza, trafficked in the sales of Nicaraguan blood to hospitals overseas. "Stories circulated in Managua that corpses found murdered by Somoza's death squads were also discovered to have been drained of blood."

Anastasio Somoza Debayle

JOSEF STALIN (1878-1953) SOVIET UNION

Son of a shoemaker, Josef Stalin began his political career as a terrorist and bank robber, attained supreme power in 1929, and didn't relinquish it until his death. Fellow despot Vladimir Lenin warned against him on his deathbed. Stalin's wife committed suicide in despair over his brutishness. Stalin observed that "the death of a man is a tragedy, the death of a thousand is a statistic." Having attained the summit of power over the peoples of the Soviet Socialist Republics, Stalin initiated a cycle of pogroms and purges that were to continue throughout his career. Cunning but paranoid, he wanted to wipe out an entire class of agrarian peasants called Kulaks; forcibly evicted from their farms en masse, the majority were shot or removed to penal camps. By his own estimation, Stalin exterminated 10,000,000 of them. Next Stalin went after "undependable workers," expunging 160,000 petty bureaucrats, party officials, civil servants, and clerical personnel. Ultimately, Stalin applied his purges to intellectuals, army staff, and anyone else who might fail to prove an ideal "new" man or woman. As a result 10,000,000 citizens wound up in the Siberian concentration camps known as "gulags." Stalin opened a phase known as The Great Terror, in which he held show trials and accused former comrades of treason. When, at the conclusion of the Second World War, 3,000,000 Russian citizens were repatriated, Stalin immediately executed the majority and sent the rest to the prisons. In his last years he became increasingly obsessed with fears of assassination or usurpation. He insisted that his food be tasted in his presence and slept in a different bed every night. Wherever he went, he had a favorite armchair taken with him, he was afraid that any other chair might contain needles in the seat that had been dipped in poison. By the time of his death he had expunged 20,000,000 persons.

Josef Stalin

VALENTINE STRASSER (1967-) SIERRA LEONE

Became head of state when he seized power at the age of twenty-five. After being ousted in a coup four years later (in 1996), he became unemployed and dependent on his family and friends for support; he is currently living on the dole at his mother's home in a suburb of the capitol, Freetown.

> Manuel Noriega, former President of Panama, was an avowed Buddhist and a confirmed cocaine addict!

ALFREDO STROESSNER (1912-2006) PARAGUAY

Such was the economic development of Paraguay under the stewardship of "El Gran Lider," Alfredo Stroessner, that dirt roads fringed the presidential palace. Under Stroessner, communists were dropped from planes to feed the piranhas or dismembered by chain saw. The face of "El Gran Lider" was posted everywhere and radio stations began the day with the *Don Alfredo Polka*, followed by the message, "The constitutional president of the republic, General Alfredo Stroessner, salutes the Paraguayan people and wishes them a prosperous day." Stroessner-governed Paraguay was a "throwaway country that nobody gives a rat's ass about," according to a US State Department official. Stroessner's sons were Freddy, who had snorted so much coke and drunk so much alcohol that he was a cirrhosing vegetable—a drooling zombie who was in and out of institutions—and Gustavo, a ruthless homosexual degenerate. Stroessner's Paraguay was a seething swirl of contraband and corruption, including Brazilian baby smuggling, where "pyragues" (hairy soles), the government spies, were ubiquitous and the prison conditions were subhuman—they've been described as the worst dungeons in the world, where prisoners broke stones twelve hours a day, Sundays and public holidays included; lived in huts where they slept and ate on the floor, surviving on starvation diets; and where, in addition to other torture methods, one favorite was submerging until near drowning in baths of human excrement. Upon escorting a foreign dignitary to the airport, Stroessner unzipped the fly of his trousers, and urinated on the wheel of the airplane—a colonel smartly jumped to attention, nudged the dignitary, and exclaimed "What a democrat, our president!" When Stroessner's procurers were not scouring the countryside for eight-to-twelve-year-old girls, "The Tyrannosaur"—Stroessner's whispered nickname—cruised the streets of Asuncion himself, in search of muchachitas—nymphets; they were his elixir, a tonic for his old age. Aides would abduct a schoolgirl of his choosing and offer a bribe to her parents; if they refused, the girl was kidnapped; if she did not cooperate, she was drugged; if she got pregnant, she was treated by the finest doctors at the best hospital. One of Stroessner's conquests was the 15-year-old daughter of the director of the national cement company. As part of the seduction, she and her brother got a trip to Disney World. When the muchachitas grew up, he lost interest in them and gave them to his lieutenants. Stroessner visited his mistress every Thursday; he had been involved with her mother first, then started with her when she was fourteen.

Alfredo Stroessner

HUGO BANZER SUAREZ (1926-2002) BOLIVIA

Bolivians refer to Banzer's term in office as the *Banzerato*, a period which witnessed the voluntary departure of thousands of citizens, while others less fortunate were arrested, tortured, and killed. Allegedly, during the seven-year span of Banzer's governance, thousands of political prisoners were incarcerated in "the horror chambers" occupying the basement of the Interior Ministry building. Neither high-ranking generals nor one former president were exempt from consideration: All were killed under questionable circumstances at the height of the *Banzerato*. Banzer enjoys another dubious distinction: He officiated during the Water Wars of 2000, achieving no resolution.

SUHARTO (1921-2008) INDONESIA

His "Berkeley mafia" was so named because of his nepotism and favoritism towards cronies and colleagues from University of California, Berkeley. He called himself the "Father of Development," while his inner circle amassed fabulous wealth—the World Bank estimating that 20 to 30 percent of the country's development budget was embezzled during his rule.

FERENC SZÁLASI (1897-1946) HUNGARY

For three fatal months, Ferenc Szálasi was the leader of the National Socialist Arrow Cross Party-Hungarist Movement and the "Leader of the Nation" being both Head of State and Prime Minister of the Kingdom of Hungary's "Government of National Unity." Szálasi's earliest involvement with full-time politics coincided with his creation of the Party of National Will, a radical, right-wing nationalistic group of which his Arrow Cross Party was a later offshoot. Szálasi was also a strong proponent of "Hungarism," advocating the expansion of

Hungarian territory to the borders of Greater Hungary as it was prior to a 1920 treaty which had reduced the country's area by 72%. During the early 1940s, Hitler's Germany protected Szálasi and, in 1944, by means of Operation Panzerfaust, absorbed Hungary as a client state with Szálasi at the helm. The Germans continued to deport Jews, but Szálasi resisted, because of the drain on manpower. In response to the situation, he created the International Ghetto in Budapest, effectively confining Jews to neutral territory. Meanwhile Szálasi shipped staple goods to Germany and conscripted Hungarians to be pitted in battle against the oncoming Red Army. Szálasi kept power for 163 days, until the Russian forces were encircling Budapest, and he absconded with his life. He turned up first in Vienna, and later Munich. After the war, he was captured and repatriated to Hungary, tried by the People's Tribunal in Budapest, sentenced to death for war crimes and high treason, and hanged.

Ferenc Szálasi

Totalitarian China launched a campaign to collect and slaughter dogs to prepare the country for the Olympic Games. Chinese officials wanted no dog poop on the streets. Vendors sell butchered dogs as "fragrant meat."

T

TAMERLANE (1336-1405) MONGOLIA

Tamerlane, AKA Timur the Vicious, the notorious Mongol conqueror, on the pretext that he was abiding by the Koran, massacred 2,000,000 men, women, and children upon invading India in 1397. He built a pyramid of 90,000 human heads before the walls of Delhi to sway that besieged city. He used tents of different colors to threaten worse disasters each day if the men under his siege did not capitulate. When he won, he used the head of the conquered general as a polo ball. Tamerlane was a wicked warmonger with a savage sadistic streak; he left nothing in his wake but rubble. He had towers or pyramids of skulls erected for his enjoyment and had thousands of opponents bricked up alive. On another time he hurled all his prisoners off a cliff to their deaths.

Tamerlane

Before his overthrow in 1974, Haile Selassie is said to have stolen Ethiopia's crown jewels and at least $80 million, which the government is still trying to recover.

TOMYRIS (?-530 BC) SCYTHIA

Scythian queen of the Massagetaean tribe who swore revenge for the death of her son against the all-powerful king of the Persians, Cyrus the Great. Ordinarily only scalping their defeated enemies, Tomyris' Scythians, capturing Cyrus, decapitated him, and Tomyris pickled his lopped-off head in a goatskin bag filled with blood, saying "Since you are so blood-thirsty, I will give you all the blood you can drink!"

TARQUIN (564 BC-505 BC) ROME

Lucius Tarquinius Superbus, or "Tarquin," as he has come down through history, murdered his way to the throne of pre-caesarian Rome and mounted a campaign of preemptive terror against everyone who might conceivably challenge him; His regime was so vicious and so draconian in its severity that Tarquin was despised by the entire populace. When Tarquin's son raped a noblewoman who subsequently committed suicide, her husband raised an army by which Tarquin was unseated and expulsed.

CHARLES TAYLOR (1948-) LIBERIA

Charles McArthur Ghankay Taylor was the 22nd President of Liberia. Educated in the United States before returning to Liberia to work in the government of Samuel Doe, he was caught embezzling $1 million intended for the purchase of machine parts and of transferring the funds to an American bank account. Fearing prosecution, he fled Liberia for the United States, where he was apprehended on an extradition warrant and jailed in a house of corrections; he fought extradition because he feared assassination by Liberian agents. He was defended by former US attorney general Ramsey Clark. He escaped from prison and made his way to Libya where he underwent guerilla training, becoming Moammar Qaddafi's protégé, then traveled to the Ivory Coast where he established a base of operations from which to launch an uprising to overthrow the Doe regime. Doe's capture and execution sparked a civil war with seven different factions in contention. In the midst of this chaos, Taylor gave diamond mining rights to American televangelist Pat Robertson who used his Operation Blessing relief effort cargo planes to transport heavy mining equipment to his new Liberian mines even though Robertson assured his viewers that he was sending emergency supplies to genocide victims in Rwanda. When the civil war ended, Taylor put himself forward as a presidential candidate using the slogan, "He killed my ma, he killed my pa, but I will vote for him." Elected to the presidency, Taylor set up a special branch of the national police called the Anti-Terrorist Unit, which effectively served him as a private army. During the Sierra Leone civil strife, when Taylor was accused of exchanging blood diamonds for smuggled weapons, he appeared on television with his spiritual advisor dressed in white robes, and begged God for forgiveness, while denying all charges. The Second Liberian Civil War broke out when rebel groups backed by neighboring Guinea and Ivory Coast surged into Liberia from both north and south, leaving Taylor in control of only one third of the country. As the United States moved warships into view of the coast, Taylor resigned and handed power to Vice President Blah. Taylor then flew to Nigeria, where the Nigerian government provided a seaside compound for him and his entourage in Calabar. When the United States offered a $2 million reward for Taylor, he vanished. From Nigeria, he tried to slip into Cameroon, but was detected and detained at the border, using a Range Rover containing large amounts of heroin and cash. Deported to Sierra Leone to stand trial for war crimes and crimes against humanity,

Taylor was found guilty on all counts. During the trial, a former military commander testified that "Charles Taylor celebrated his newfound status during the civil war by ordering human sacrifice, including the killings of opponents and allies perceived to have betrayed him," and by "having a pregnant woman buried alive in sand," and "forcing cannibalism on his soldiers in order to terrorize their enemies." In all, Taylor was convicted of eleven counts of aiding and abetting war crimes and crimes against humanity, including: terrorizing the local population and collective punishments; acts of terrorism and unlawful killings including murder, violence to life, health and physical or mental well-being of persons; sexual violence, including rape, sexual slavery, and outrages upon personal dignity; physical violence, including violence to health and physical and mental well-being of persons, in particular cruel treatment and other inhumane acts; use of child soldiers, including conscripting or enlisting children under the age of fifteen years into armed forces or groups, or using them to participate actively in hostilities; abductions and forced labor; enslavement; looting; and pillage.

THAN SHWE (1933-) BURMA

Mysterious Burmese leader so reclusive that many of his compatriots don't even know what he looks like. High school dropout who became commander of the armed forces and, in the wake of abortive elections, was thrust into the limelight as head of state. Regarding Than's rapid ascent to such lofty heights, a government insider waggishly commented that Than's talent for upward mobility was due to "his ability to bore everyone else into submission." The man Than was replacing had smashed a democratization movement and snuffed out 3,000 protesters. Brutal and remorseless, Than himself shows small regard for human rights and has no compunction about granting approval for dissidents, journalists, and even Buddhist monks to be beaten, jailed, tortured, or executed. Free press and speech do not exist in Burma. The security apparatus favors rape, torture, summary execution, and disappearances to keep the citizenry in line. Recent protests provoked a severe crack-down, which left hundreds dead. Than's disastrous fiscal policies have kept Burma one of the world's most impoverished nations. Highly superstitious, Than moved the national capital on the advice of an astrologer. A favorite psychic is "a tiny, hunched, deaf-mute in her mid-forties." Alarmed by anti-government protests, Than Shwe's wife and pets have fled the country.

TIBERIUS (42 BC-37 AD) ROME

At his imperial pleasure palace on the Isle of Capri, Emperor Tiberius relaxed by swimming in a beautiful blue grotto filled with small boys and girls. These children, whom he called his "minnows," had been specially trained to swim underwater and nibble at his private parts, so as to stimulate his flagging sexual energies; those who annoyed him as he was vacationing at the villa were thrown from the edge of Capri's sheer cliffs onto the rocky shoreline far below.

JOSIP BROZ TITO (1892-1980) YUGOSLAVIA

Malignant marshal of a Soviet satellite state, Tito started life as a metalworker before moving up through ranks of the Communist Party and emerging, by the end of World War II, as Yugoslavia's virtual dictator. By way of purges, plots, and secret police, he held onto power for decades.

TITUS (39-89) ROME

Military commander and Roman emperor whose many martial adventures included the conquest of Judaea and the sack of Jerusalem, during which 2,000,000 Jewish lives, young and old, were lost—half as a result of the starvation, plague, and other ravages of the long siege, half cut down by the Roman phalanxes. During the storming of Jerusalem, the magnificent temple, the Hebrew holy of holies, was burned to the ground. For thirty relentless days, the Roman mercenaries pillaged, plundered, and mutilated the city, putting to the sword all who resisted and just as many who didn't, then enslaving the wholly subjugated survivors.

HIDEKI TOJO (1884-1948) JAPAN

Maniacal, white-gloved Japanese nationalist known as "The Razor," prime minister of Japan during the Second World War, and instigator of Japanese aggression against China, Russia, and the United States who, with the complicity and approval of Emperor Hirohito, was responsible for innumerable atrocities: the Rape of Nanking, during which Japanese troops slaughtered 300,000 Chinese men, women, children, and infants; the Sook Ching Massacre in Singapore, during which the Japanese killed 50,000 more; and the systematic slaughter of another three million non-combatants throughout greater China. On the domestic front, he formed the *Kempai Tai*—the Japanese Counterespionage and Secret Military Police—which was omnipresent and omniscient in Japanese society and, during the War, in all occupied territories. Their numbers in 1945 were estimated at 70,000 members on the home islands alone and twice that number in occupied territories. The Kempai Tai exercised censorship and controlled propaganda, regulated sales of arms, explosives, and drugs, and the Secret Military Field Police had the power to arrest any army rank three times their senior, administering punishment on the spot. Under Tojo's inhumane leadership, one of the most infamous incidents of the War occurred: the Bataan Death March, during which American and Filipino prisoners of war were forced to march for days without food or water and were bayoneted if they stopped to rest or took a drink at a stagnant pool, and had to sleep in filthy, cramped, and overcrowded conditions, amongst their own excretions. Many did not survive and many others died at their destination. Tojo oversaw the entire conduct of the Asian and Pacific Wars, from the attack on the American fleet at Pearl Harbor to the last ditch fanaticism of the kamikazes. In 1945, realizing defeat, he attempted suicde

Hideki Tojo

but failed, and was captured, convicted of war crimes, and sentenced to death by hanging, unrepentant to the end.

AHMED SEKOU TOURÉ (1922-1984) GUINEA

When Ghana's president and fellow strongman Kwame Nkrumah was ousted from office, Touré granted him asylum in Guinea and made him his co-president. When a Guinean delegation was imprisoned in Ghana, after the overthrow of Nkrumah, Touré blamed Washington. He feared that the Central Intelligence Agency was plotting against his own regime. Over time, Touré's increasing paranoia led him to arrest large numbers of suspected political opponents and imprison them in camps, such as the notorious Camp Boiro National Guard Barracks. Some 50,000 people are believed to have been killed under the regime of Touré in concentration camps like Camp Boiro. Tens of thousands of Guinean dissidents sought refuge in exile. Touré died in 1984 while undergoing cardiac treatment at a clinic in Cleveland, Ohio; he had been rushed to the United States after being stricken in Saudi Arabia the previous day. On hearing the news, the armed forces seized power in Guinea, denouncing the last years of Touré's rule as a "bloody and ruthless dictatorship." The constitution was suspended, the National Assembly dissolved, and the PDG abolished. The leader of the coup, Colonel Lansana Conté, assumed the presidency, heading the Military Committee for National Recovery and about 1,000 political prisoners were freed. In 1985 Conté took advantage of an alleged coup attempt to execute several of Sekou Touré's close associates, including the former commander of Camp Boiro.

MOUSSA TRAORÉ (1936-) MALI

Moussa Traoré was President for Life of the Republic of Mali from 1979 to 1991, when he was brought down by popular protests and military take-over. He was twice condemned to death in the 1990s, but pardoned on both occasions and freed in 2002. He has since retired from political life. From Traoré's first days in office, political activity was banned and a police state was put into operation assisted by a network of informers. When a drought hit Mali, aid money was misappropriated. In 1979, Traoré created the Democratic Union of Malian People, a single permitted political party, and stood for election, which, as the only candidate, he won with 99% of the vote. At around the same time, he created two organizations with compulsory membership: the National Union of Malian Women and the Malian National Youth Union. Traoré crushed student demonstrations and tortured to death their leaders. Students, even children, played an increasing role in protest marches, and homes and businesses of those associated with the regime were ransacked by crowds. In 1991 a huge demonstration was quashed. Days later a military coup deposed Traoré and he was condemned to death for killing around three hundred pro-democracy demonstrators, but his sentence was later commuted.

> The motto of Paraguay under the administration of Supreme Leader Alfredo Stroessner was, "By Reason or by Force!"

RAFAEL TRUJILLO (1891–1961) DOMINICAN REPUBLIC

A five foot tall dandy who wore $10,000 suits, elevator shoes, and saturated himself with perfumes, and who decreed that no man could appear on the streets of the capital city without a jacket and tie and would be arrested if barefoot. If a citizen had no shoes, he could rent a pair at the city's edge. He designated himself "The Benefactor." His underlings referred to him as "Chief." On the street he was known as "The Goat." Children fashioned bottlecaps into simulacra of the flashy medals he favored for display on his uniforms. His son-in-law was the international playboy Pofirio Rubirosa. In an election in which he won more votes than there were registered voters, he rose to assume the presidency of the Dominican Republic wearing a sash that read, "God and Trujillo." He renamed the country's tallest mountain peak after himself and changed the name of the capital to Trujillo City. Automobile license plates bore the slogan "Long Live Trujillo!" and statues of his likeness sprouted throughout the land. Residences were expected to prominently display a sign touting the slogan "God and Trujillo" and citizens were encouraged to hold membership in the country's only political party—controlled by Trujillo—and required to carry a party identification card without which they risked retribution such as being charged with vagrancy or loitering. When in the Generalissimo's presence, visitors were greeted by gun-toting bodyguards. "The 42," a goon squad of elect henchmen among his secret police, the SIM, patrolled the capital in an ominous red Packard denominated by locals as "the Chariot of Death." Disappearances, arbitrary arrest and imprisonment, and perfunctory killings were commonplace. The city of San Cristobal was designated by federal decree as "The Meritorious City" because it was his birthplace. A resplendent bantam peacock who threw enemies to the sharks, this strutting Caribbean caudillo had only an elementary school education, and had been a telegraph operator, petty thief, forger, embezzler, and cattle rustler. He had lived in the jungle as a revolutionary on the run and worked at a sugar refinery as a clerk, then as a security guard, then joined the National Police. He finagled himself into being appointed Minister of Defense. After strongarming himself into the position of president, calendars were calibrated according to the Era of Trujillo, with 1930 as the year One. Pico Duarte, at ten thousand feet, the tallest peak in the Caribbean, would be renamed Little Trujillo. Every dinner began with a toast to Trujillo. He favored Packards but also used Cadillacs. He maintained a cordon sanitaire of plausible deniability and "denounced and expunged anyone who fell short of his approval" in private or professional comportment.

"Trujillo was one of those fastidious sadists who placed the highest premium on personal grooming, polite manners, and moral uprightness. Never mind that he was the sort of tyrant who preyed on young girls throughout his country (legend would have it that some Dominican families deliberately hid their daughters away or even scarred them so they wouldn't in mid-puberty be set upon by the Benefactor). Everyone in his circle had to conform to his courtly ideals of appearance and decorum. His punctiliousness puzzled and frightened everyone. By the 1950s, some twenty years into his reign, he had massacred and raped and emptied the pockets of tens of thousands. He had a secret police force, the SIM, run by a half-German, half-Dominican named Jonny Abbes Garcia, a pudgy, vicious killer who oversaw a variety of operations of intimidation, extortion, murder, and torture both at home and abroad to protect trujillismo from its oceans of enemies. The SIM killed with both an electric chair and a block-and-tackle suspended over a vat of boiling oil. And he had as well his pen—and access to all media distributed in the country. With the tools of physical and psychological terror, he forced the entire country to knuckle under. And it would be hard in some cases to say whether the tortures inflicted by Abbes Garcia or the genteel tyranny of the 'Foro Publico' were more degrading." His son Ramfis, enveloped by a retinue of bodyguards, secretaries, aides, and hangers-on, was regarded by professional psychiatrists as psychotic: He was "mopey, given to broody, boozy torpors—he was a mess." Trujillo aspired to control the entire island of Hispaniola, which the Dominican Republic shares with Haiti. In order to prosecute this aim, he tried to spark a war with Haiti, and he made an assassination attempt on at least two successive Haitian presidents. In an incident known as the Parsley Massacre (so called because Dominican soldiers who carried it out chose their victims by first asking them to say the Spanish word parsley—*perejil*—whose letter "r" was difficult to pronounce; if they failed this test, they were sliced to pieces with machetes) in what came to be known as El Corte—"The Cutting"—men, women and children were indiscriminately butchered. His military forces attacked Haitians who had encroached along both sides of the border, killing an estimated 15,000 to 30,000 civilians. He detested Haitians, and this was his way of discouraging illegal immigration. When Fidel Castro overthrew Fulgencio Batista in Cuba, Trujillo took him in and sheltered him, but held him hostage and wouldn't let him leave until he had paid several million dollars in tribute. Castro tried to unseat Trujillo and vice versa; neither prevailed. He enjoyed the same relationship with Venezuelan president Romulo Betancourt; they hated each other and each sponsored plots to depose the other, including an assassination attempt mounted by Trujillo against the Venezuelan leader. Meanwhile, Trujillo routinely ordered the murder of his political opponents and of anyone who criticized him. His unpopularity increased, both at home and abroad and, eventually, a car in which he was riding was ambushed on a quiet country road, and he was cut down by a hail of gunfire. More than sixty bullets had struck the vehicle—curiously, it was an Oldsmobile and not a Packard or Cadillac as were his preferences. He was quite a clotheshorse and maintained a wardrobe of two thousand suits and ten thousand cravats. He accumulated great wealth and owned numerous estates scattered all over the country. A famous line was created when US Secretary of State Cordell Hull said of Trujillo, "He may be a son of a bitch, but he's *our* son of a bitch!" Trujillo's private yacht, *Angelita*, was the largest and most luxurious in the world at the time.

Rafael Trujillo

TZU-HSI (1834-1908) CHINA

Tzu-hsi, whose formal title was "Motherly Auspicous Orthodox Heaven-Blessed Prosperous All-Nourishing Brightly Manifest Calm Sedate Perfect Long-lived Respectful Reverend Worshipful Illustrious Exalted Empress Dowager," was a five-foot-tall Chinese imperial concubine famed for her beauty and charm, who became empress of China in the latter part of the nineteenth century. At seventeen, Tzu-hsi, meaning kindly and virtuous, entered the service of the Chinese emperor as a concubine. When he elected to sleep with her, in order to prevent any weapons being brought to the room, an escort of eunuchs left her naked at the foot of the bed. Of all the emperor's wives and concubines, only Tzu-hsi bore him a son. This fact resulted in the immediate exaltation of her prestige and position and her eventual accession to the status of Empress of the Western Palace. Her relations with the Emperor, however, were somewhat less than ideal. Apart from his suffering from venereal disease, she regarded him as weak and ineffectual and their relationship was strained by a continual power struggle. The Boxer Rebellion of 1900 signalled a turning point in her reign. The Boxer Rebellion was named after the secret society of the "Righteous and Harmonious Fists" who were poor Chinese who blamed Westerners and their imperialism for their poor standard of living. First organized in 1898, they may have been tacitly supported by Tzu-hsi's government. The Boxers attacked Western missionaries and merchants, as well as the compound in Peking where foreigners lived, beginning a siege which lasted eight weeks. In the throes of the fighting, the French cathedral was burned to the ground and, in the conflagration, hundreds of men, women, and children lost their lives. Dragon Empress Tzu-hsi witnessed the fire from a hillside nearby, then ordered a halt to the bombardment because the noise was giving her a headache. "While the red-turbaned rioters she championed rampaged around the Celestial City yelling "Burn! Burn! Burn! Kill! Kill! Kill!" she was engaged in painting delicate designs of bamboo on silk or arranging exquisite

189

water picnics on the palace lake. While Christians were massacred, thousands of Chinese converts among them, she tended her four-inch-long fingernails, shielded with jade, and tottered round her gardens in jewel-encrusted shoes. Let no one escape..." she had ordered, "so that my empire may be purged." At length, the 19,000 troops of the allied armies of the Western imperialist Powers captured Peking and ended the siege. Tzu-hsi decided to flee the city with the emperor. The Boxer Rebellion was over. At least 250 foreigners had been killed and China had to accept a humiliating peace settlement. In 1901, she returned to the city with a whole new outlook. She was now in favor of modernizing China and making moral and social reforms. One of her major reforms was to outlaw slicing, a practice of killing people with thousands of small cuts. She considered the idea of constructing a railroad system in China but rejected it because she said it would be "too noisy." In 1908, Tzu-hsi suffered a stroke. She was buried in sumptuous splendor, opulently smothered in diamonds. In 1928, revolutionaries dynamited her tomb and looted it while desecrating her body.

U

JORGE UBICO (1878-1946) GUATEMALA

Jorge Ubico y Castañeda was Guatemalan dictator from 1931 to 1944. Once in office, he set in motion a program of efficiency and austerity reinforced by dictatorial prerogatives. He forged an unholy alliance with the United Fruit Company with the intention of fostering economic development and favored the American firm with many perquisites and incentives such as tax exemptions and exclusive use of railroad and port facilities. Ubico fancied himself a "second Napoleon" and was obsessed with this eccentric notion. His admiration for the French military genius was boundless. Although he was heavier and considerably taller than his hero, Ubico believed that he resembled Bonaparte, and liked to pose in his ostentatious general's uniform so that the resemblance might be better appreciated. He surrounded himself with busts and portraits of Napoleon, regularly remarking on the similarities between them, and dubbed himself "the Napoleon of the Tropics." An observer at the time noted that "he militarized numerous political and social institutions—including the post office, schools, and symphony orchestras—and placed military officers in charge of many government posts. He frequently travelled around the country performing 'inspections' in dress uniform followed by a military escort, a mobile radio station, an official biographer, and cabinet members." Ubico's obnoxious policies and haughty demeanor led to a broad-based insurrection and, in 1944, Ubico stepped down amidst a general strike and nationwide protests. When congress convened to hold an election to select a provisional president, soldiers kept everyone at gunpoint and forced them to vote for General

Ponce, an alcoholic and an Ubico puppet. Ponce took orders from Ubico and retained many of the officials from Ubico's administration. The repressive tactics continued. Ubico died in exile in New Orleans.

V

VALERIAN (195-260) ROME

Roman emperor who, along with his wife, was taken captive by invading Persian emperor Shapur I. In order to humiliate Valerian, Shapur used him as a footstool to mount his horse and issued an edict granting any of his subjects, to the lowest leper or pariah, and including animals, to sodomize him at will. After his death, by Shapur's command, Valerian's skin was stripped off, colored with dyes, and used to decorate Shapur's chambers. So much for the grandeur that was Rome...

GETÚLIO VARGAS (1882-1954) BRAZIL

Getúlio Dornelles Vargas served as both dictator and as democratically elected president of Brazil for a span of eighteen years. He oversaw an authoritarian corporatist regime known as the *Estado Novo* ("New State") that established state monopolies for oil, mining, steelmaking, chemicals, and automobiles. The impact and implications of his policies were still resonating at the time of the Brazilian Economic Miracle of the 1960s–1980s. Legend holds that Vargas was in love with glamorous international fashion model Aimee de Heeren and that he pursued a relationship with her that was a state secret. Heeren was admired by other notable statesmen, including the Massachusetts Kennedys. Although wealthy, Vargas was something of a populist in the Juan Peron mold, and his principal rivals were oligarchs intent on a smokescreen government consisting of a façade democracy. Under the jurisdiction of the New State, Vargas managed dissent through press and mail censorship. Comparisons between Vargas' New State and European police states began to surface when Vargas began encouraging the spread of fascist support

193

groups in Brazil. One such movement, Integralism, "adopted Fascist and Nazi symbolism and salutes and offered Vargas a new constituency. A green-shirted paramilitary organization directly financed by Mussolini and Hitler, Integralism's propaganda campaigns were borrowed directly from Nazi models that espoused fanatical nationalism and 'Christian virtues.' Under the Estado Novo, Vargas abolished political parties, imposed censorship, established a centralized police force, and filled prisons with political dissidents, while evoking a sense of nationalism that transcended class and bound the masses to the state." By 1954, Vargas had reached an ideological impasse with the military that could not be bridged. When he learned that ambitious elements in the Brazilian military intended to demand that he step down, he committed suicide by shooting himself in the chest with a revolver at the Catete Palace where his nightshirt with a bullet hole in the breast is kept on public display.

JORGE VIDELA (1925-) ARGENTINA

Jorge Rafael Videla Redondo was the *de facto* President of Argentina from 1976 to 1981. He came to power in a coup d'état that deposed Isabel Martínez de Perón and, during a period of upheaval that pitted terrorist attacks by leftist subversives against kidnappings, torture, and assassination by right wing death squads, the junta headed by Videla felt justified in taking severe measures to stabilize the nation in the midst of what they called the "internal war." All political power was concentrated in the hands of the nine-man junta, and all key government posts were held by loyal military officers. After restitution of democratic government in Argentina, Videla was prosecuted for large-scale human rights abuses and crimes against humanity that took place under his rule, including "abductions, forced disappearance, widespread torture and extrajudicial murder of activists, political opponents (either real, suspected or alleged) as well as their families, at secret concentration camps." Accusations included the "theft of many babies born during the captivity of their mothers at the illegal detention centers." In 2010, Videla was given a life sentence in a civilian prison for causing the deaths of thirty-one persons arrested during his coup d'état. At minimum, 9,000 and perhaps up to 30,000 Argentinians "disappeared" and probably fell victim to government-directed homicide. Videla himself confirmed that at least 8,000 Argentinians were "murdered by his regime and their bodies hidden or destroyed to prevent protests at home and abroad." The Assembly for Human Rights believes that 12,261 people were killed or disappeared during the "National Reorganization Process." Democracy was restored in 1983, and Videla was put on trial and found guilty. In handing down the sentence, the judge declared that Videla was "a manifestation of state terrorism."

VITELLIUS (15-69) ROME

Vicious Aulus Vitellius started on the ladder to success as a child prostitute. He was said to have been the catamite of four libidinous emperors before him and his capacity for lewdness, lasciviousness, and debauchery made him a favorite at court. He is remembered for having enlarged the inventory of Spintrian postures with highly imaginative novelties. When, as emperor, he could indulge his every caprice, he gave himself over to laziness and self-indulgence, and was so fond of eating and drinking that he became an incorrigible glutton, so obese that he had difficulty walking. He liked to feast four times a day and thought nothing of sending the Roman navy far and wide to procure exotic tidbits on which to dine. His body was obscenely fat, with a massive paunch engendered by incessant banqueting and lubricated by fervid drinking binges. For his daily banquets, he invited himself to the houses of different nobles on a rotating schedule. Each of these meals, at others' expense, was required to cost a minimum of $8,000; at one sitting, 2,000 fish and 7,000 gamebirds were served. One of Vitellius' favorite dishes was called

Minerva's Shield: The recipe called for the brains, livers, tongues, and innards of lampreys, flamingos, pheasants, peacocks, and pikes. He was exceptionally superstitious. He is even reported to have poisoned his own mother in order to fulfill a prophecy that his reign would be a long one if his mother preceded him in death. Vitellius banished astrologers from Rome. Some of them responded by circulating a prophecy to the effect that he would perish before the date announced to enforce his banishment decree. Any astrologers Vitellius came across were put to the sword. As Vespasian, Emperor of the East, arrived in Rome to claim the insignia of office after defeating Vitellius' armies in battle, guards snatched Vitellius from a janitor's closet where he had been hiding and marched him to the Gemonian Stairs as crowds pelted him with dung. At the top of the steps he was strangled and his body thrown into the Tiber. "Can it be that I was once your emperor?" was his final utterance.

VLAD TEPES (1431-1476) ROMANIA

Inspiration for the legend of Dracula. For executing enemies, he favored impalement on stakes, and drank his victims' blood. On one occasion he sat down to dinner surrounded by a large number of slowly dying victims. When one of his guests, sickened by the stench and the screams, made the mistake of complaining, Vlad had him impaled so that "he could be above the smell." He put down a rebellion by making it known that the bodies of plotters would be fed to the crabs, and the crabs then force fed to their families. He also forced wives to eat the roasted bodies of their husbands and made parents cannibalize their children. When a party of visiting diplomats failed to remove their hats in his presence, he ordered the hats to be nailed to their heads, and their epaulets nailed to their shoulders.

W

WILLIAM THE CONQUEROR (1027-1087) ENGLAND

A relentless and all-pervading lust for conquest was indeed the motivating principle in the life of William I, more popularly known as William the Conqueror. Wars of aggression, expansion, and territorial acquisition were his stock in trade. He raised a gigantic, rag-tag army of mercenary riff-raff, with which he met and defeated King Harold at the Battle of Hastings. After dispatching Harold to his heavenly reward, he marched his motley army on a zigzagging rampage across England burning villages, destroying crops, and slaying menfolk and cattle, in a savage wave of medieval genocide. Ever widening the swath he cut across Britain, he subdued everything in his path. Once he had pacified the populace, he set in place a special brand of feudalism facilitated by a *Domesday Book* which cataloged every parcel of land in Britain, probably with a view to appropriating it or, at least, with a view to extracting tribute from each and every inhabitant from whom he demanded complete and utter subservience, in accord with the precedent he had set: a mandate requiring absolute loyalty to himself the king, above all other considerations, including the church.

WU CHAO (625-705) CHINA

Through a series of royal deaths and twists and turns in the dynastic succession, Wu Chao rose from the status of a thirteen-year-old junior concubine in the Chinese royal court to attain the position of empress. At first she wisely managed the Censorate and Councils of State and Military Affairs but, at length, she got entangled in court intrigues and scandals involving her amorous liaisons and her son was prevailed upon to persuade her to abdicate. No other woman in history, except for Catherine the Great or England's Elizabeth I, has held sway over so vast an empire.

X

XERXES (519 BC–465 BC) PERSIA

King Xerxes of Persia, halting at the seashore in the presence of his entourage and an entire army, instructed his soldiers to horsewhip the obstreperous ocean because it made too much noise.

Xerxes

Paul, the "Mad Czar" of Russia, sent off 400 troops on a 2,000 mile trek to Siberia (none was ever seen again) because one of them, during inspection, was found to have a button missing from his uniform.

Y

YUAN SHIKAI (1859-1916) CHINA

Ill-fated president of China who rose meteorically and rapidly fell from grace. Chosen to rebuild China's army following the Sino-Japanese War, Yuan further impressed the empress dowager Tzu-hsi when his division was the only one to emerge intact from the Boxer Rebellion. In the shadow of her death and the demise of the Qing Dynasty, Yong became China's first president of the newborn republic. He was impatient with the workings of representative government and schemed to have his leading rival murdered. He plummeted further into disfavor when he pronounced himself Emperor. The tide of public opinion turned against him, once-loyal subordinates abandoned him, and he succumbed to uremia, aged fifty-six. His death would open the door to the warlord era, an unstable period during which control of China was fragmented among competing military cliques, each vying for the upper hand.

SHAKA ZULU (1787-1828) SOUTH AFRICA

Emperor and Chief Paramount of the Zulus, the "Great Elephant" and native lord of the South African Empire, he maintained a private harem of twelve hundred women, whom he called "sisters." "Human beings were, to him, bugs to be crushed at will: He rounded up three hundred women and asked each if she owned a cat—regardless of the answers, he had them killed; he slashed open the bellies of one hundred women just to see inside; he executed 7,000 of his own warriors purely out of spite; he developed the "horned buffalo" infantry formation, which he and his army of 40,000 marauders used to devastating effect, wiping out 2,000,000 lives during their sweeping and remorseless *mfecanes*, or "crushings."

THE GLAMOUR OF EVIL

Perhaps no character type exerts so powerful a fascination on the imagination as the villain. Villains have existed in every epoch and every era, and the history of villainy is inseparable from the problem of evil itself.

The villain's allure is undeniable, and the profound imprint he has left on legend and literature far from accidental. The dictator archetype is the quintessential villain, and the theatricality of his persona is unparalleled. Surrounded by pomp and ceremony, as well as by a retinue of sycophants—toadying officials, surly bureaucrats, groveling courtiers and government grotesques, underlings and lackeys of every stripe—he is a thespian enacting a role. His minutest movements are scrupulously monitored and analyzed, his attire is a symbolic uniform or an elaborate costume stealing a page from the most flamboyant fashion sketchbook. Almost invariably, he is an individual in whom the powers of evil are exalted.

Whether an unmitigated menace or a man of reasonable comity, his is a personality apart—stern, forbidding, perverse. He is half-monster, half-god. Men tremble in their boots and women pee in their panties at his approach and, in the face of his obloquies, faint dead away. He is a murderous fiend who can snuff out a life with the snap of his fingers. He is a lecherous satyr whose lubricious escapades are bruited far and wide. He may be the most stylish and suave of bluebloods or the most oafish of vulgarians. He may be perceived as knave or national savior. His reputation is the product of whispered gossip filtered through a funnel of trembling rumor and terrified innuendo. The pantheon of his partners in crime is vast and seemingly perpetual inasmuch as, like weeds, when one is cut down, three more spring up in its place. His entire zeitgeist is a perfect expression of a curious paradox, which has passed into universal folklore: "If you commit murder, you go to jail; if you commit a million murders, you're a national hero."

The dictator, for the most part, is not mistaken for a hero. His villainy is recognized by all of those not held in his favor, and by many who are. Somehow, through some mysterious process, no matter how many or how grave his felonies, he remains a celebrated figure; even, in some measure, a focus of admiration and awe. This phenomenon can undoubtedly be attributed to the mere fact that he has had the audacity to seize power over his meeker fellows and to aspire to rule over and dominate them. The beguilement of the world by this strong personality can be equated to a fascination with what can only be called *the glamour of evil*.

This strange force has manifested itself in an even more curious phenomenon: *dictator chic*—the commercialization and commodification of the dictator into an array of merchandise including movies, books, apparel, and foodstuffs.

While, in the late nineteenth century, casual escapist novels introduced the relatively mild-mannered, cutesy-poo rulers of such imaginary kingdoms as Graustark and Ruritania, diluted for palatability as innocuous romantic fantasy, the twentieth century brought episodic soap operas chronicling the succession of the early Caesars and a whole new Latin American literary genre devoted to the eternal dictator theme. Today, the dictator is a routine character in contemporary films, and television newsreels of toppled tyrants make for titillating table talk.

The Japanese rising sun and the Nazi swastika have become part of pop iconography, there are soft drinks and candy bars featuring heroes of the Russian Revolution and dictator statuary and memorabilia are sold online. Andy Warhol's campy portrait of Chairman Mao—the Mao who killed forty-five million of his fellow Chinese citizens—is displayed in museums and featured in contemporary art catalogs while the glowering face of Ayatollah Khomeini may appear on a cereal box in Iran. Dictator kitsch is everywhere, from the brand of condoms named after the Egyptian pharaoh Ramses to billboards, propaganda posters, confections, postage stamps, currency, public statuary, souvenir figurines, buttons, and toys. Recent eBay auctions have featured Mussolini medallions, Juan and Eva Peron porcelain busts, Shah of Iran medallions, five communist dictator medals—Lenin, Stalin, Mao, Ho Chi Minh, and Tito—all made in Albania, a Stalin porcelain bust, a Hitler bust, and a Stalin bas-relief.

Dictators have become a part of pop history, remembered for their eccentricities and extravagant utopian fantasies: Hitler's dream of a thousand-year Reich; Hussein's imperative to rebuild ancient Babylon; daffy Qaddafi's vision of a Pan-African Union; and so on. After their demise, they pass into a weird twilight of criminal mythology and seem unreal, like stars whose light still reaches us although they were extinguished millions of years ago.

Unfortunately, dictatorship is not a quaint artifact of another age. It has not been relegated to the shadowy mists of time. It persists all around us and its stark reality is making inroads everywhere as the tentacles of government control intrude into every corner of our private lives. Try as we may to brush aside these somber facts with gallows humor, the joke is on us...

DOGMEAT

If it is true that Man's nature is divided between the spiritual and the animal, it's a close call deciding which side has the advantage. Two hundred fifty years after the Enlightenment, Man still struggles to overcome the depredations wrought by corrupt officials, avaricious politicians, crooked financiers, mercenary advisors, and criminal gangs. The destructive effects of spent ideologies, fraudulent government policies, and bankrupt institutions all take their toll.

Best-intentioned efforts, from the Pax Romana to the League of Nations, have never saved mankind from itself. Present-day organizations such as the United Nations and Amnesty International often prove ineffective to the point of uselessness. Over the centuries, hundreds of major wars, pestilences, famines, and other disasters have plagued humanity. And when the specter of dictatorship raises its head and the land is cast in its ugly shadow, the ostrichlike majority who watch from afar bury their beaks in comfortable burrows of benign indifference.

If history is regarded as a living organism, dictators are germs— noxious microbes that cause infection. In fighting this malady, civilization has made great strides, but still has found no cure.

Populations act like sheep, susceptible to the will to power of strong individuals eager to herd them. Through deceit, propaganda, media manipulation, and other such herd mechanics, the blinded, gullible citizenry is led to slaughter.

Alas, forlorn mankind! The price of liberty is eternal vigilance. Yet despite every fealty to vigilance, humanity all too frequently finds itself hard-pressed to stay at one remove from a Morlocks and Eloi equation.

Given the ravages to which it has been subject during thousands of years of earthly habitation, it is no small miracle that the human race has managed to survive. Advances on many fronts, social and technological, must be conceded and admired. Nevertheless, backstage of the pageant of human progress lurk arch fiends hungry to play the overlord, and to ensure that, until such time as man awakes from his indolent slumber, the master/slave paradigm shall still prevail. Sadly, in the end, victimization orchestrated by villainous despots, whether agents of monarchies, oligarchies, or democracies, will undoubtedly remain all but inevitable. Man's probable fate can be summed up by one pathetic word: *dogmeat…*